THE MATCHING PAIR
Part 2
DOUBLE ACT
by
Allan Warren

BUNNYWAR BOOKS

First published in 2022
by Bunnywar Books, London

The Matching Pair - Part 2: Double Act

Cast in order of appearance:

JUDY: Early twenties, attractive, upmarket.

KATE: Late forties, good looking, sophisticated, bitchy.

ROGER: Mid thirties, handsome, intelligent.

MARK: Mid twenties, effeminate, attractive.

MATTHEW: Similar age, masculine, extremely handsome.

The action takes place in a Victorian apartment building, on the Chelsea/Fulham border in London. The year is 1973.

To Sandra

Allan Warren

ACT ONE, SCENE I

JUDY: *(The song Daydreamer sung by David Cassidy is playing, it fades as the curtain goes up to reveal a messy living room in daytime. The paint on the walls is faded, with only bright patches, where pictures used to hang. Centrestage are a pair of antique red leather armchairs and a sofa with a spring sticking out of it. Upstage left of the sofa are a stack of packing cases. Seemingly, there is no one on stage, until we hear the noise of paper rustling. JUDY appears from behind the packing cases)* It has to be...? *(JUDY is holding an old newspaper and a pencil. She looks around at the labels on the boxes and begins rummaging in one marked books. JUDY pulls out a dictionary. As she flips through the pages, JUDY walks upstage centre towards the kitchen area)* Aha, here we are, that's it! *(As JUDY puts on the kettle, the intercom buzzes. Still immersed in her crossword, JUDY walks downstage right and without answering, pushes the buzzer)* It has to be. Now let's see, seven letters. A type of Acacia tree, native to Arabia. *(JUDY begins pencilling in the crossword. The doorbell rings and JUDY opens the front door. Framed in the doorway is an elegant smartly dressed woman, in her early forties. JUDY'S mind is still on the crossword)* That's definitely it.

KATE: What is?

JUDY: *(looks up)* Shitta

KATE: Unless you're suffering from Tourettes, dear. A simple hello would have sufficed.

JUDY: I'm sorry... It's just that the Shittah has seven letters. *(KATE pushes past JUDY to the middle of the living room. KATE is wearing*

7

a matching skirt and jacket with white kid gloves)

KATE: So? Lavatory has eight, but that's no substitute for a simple hello.

JUDY: Sorry, hello.

KATE: What on earth are you going on about?

JUDY: You see, Shittah is a tree that grows in the Sinai Desert.

KATE: Yes, dear, I've heard quite enough. Honestly, you've been in Fulham for two minutes and you're already talking like a native. Around here, they all seem to be suffering from Tourettes.

JUDY: *(baffled)* It's just a word I was looking up. *(hands KATE the newspaper)* I found this old newspaper in the wardrobe; it's dated 1938, and apart from Chamberlain waving that peace offering to Germany on the front cover, it has this crossword inside. *(goes upstage to the kitchen)* Would you like some tea? I was just about to make some.

KATE: *(uses the newspaper to brush herself a clean place on the sofa)* What's that dear? *(goes to sit down, rubs her gloved hand across the edge of the sofa and then examines her glove)* No, no thanks; I have to rush off soon to have my hair washed. *(to herself)* And by the look of it, the rest of me, too! *(finally sits and then looks at the crossword)* I gave up doing these ages ago, the very day my divorce came through.

JUDY: What's Uncle Charles's divorce got to do with crosswords?

KATE: A hell of a lot! I wasted many boring years doing little else.

That was before I realised men are like tiles, even if you haven't laid them... You can still walk all over them.

JUDY: That's not very nice.

KATE: It wasn't meant to be. My dear, a word of advice. If you've come to London to live, learn more about men. They are the real puzzles, forget crosswords.

JUDY: Oh, come on! You were good at them.

KATE: Good? I was excellent! Darling, what else was a girl meant to do married to him? God, he was dull... But at least he was rich.

JUDY: You were married for what.. eight, nine years?

KATE: Yes, nine. Nine wonderful years... Of boredom! D'you know, we hardly ever went to a restaurant?

JUDY: But you love eating out?

KATE: By the time Charles got home from the office, he was too tired to go anywhere. I hated staying in, but I had no choice.

JUDY: Surely, you could have gone on your own?

KATE: Where's the fun in that? When I did venture out on my own, he'd be in a mood for days.

JUDY: It shows he obviously cared.

KATE: He cared alright... But not about me. He was just terrified I'd blow his cover. *(JUDY looks surprised)* All Charles really cared about was making money... And protecting his image.

JUDY: His image?

KATE: The one of us being a respectable, happily married couple.

JUDY: But that's exactly what you were.

KATE: *(smirks)* That was all a facade, dear. And when on the rare occasion, I did manage to slip off on my own, he'd accuse me of having a lover.

JUDY: You didn't... Did you?

KATE: A lover? *(laughs)* Oh, darling. I should have been so lucky, because he certainly wasn't one. Well, not in bed anyway. It was obvious. Early on in the marriage, for him, the idea of sex with me was abhorrent.

JUDY: Really? But I thought you were mad about each other.

KATE: Mad? Oh, yes! We were. Mad to believe that it could ever work. I always had my suspicions he was hiding something. But to be honest, darling - I didn't care! In truth, I only married him for his money. *(JUDY looks surprised)* I thought once I got the ring on my finger, it wouldn't matter if I did slip off occasionally and have a bit of fun. After all, he'd be so tied up working, totting up his finances in the City that he wouldn't notice or even care. Instead, what happens? Charles decides to sell off our house in Eaton Place and buy a large Victorian edifice in Guildford.

JUDY: Guildford?

KATE: Can you believe it? I was in strutting distance of Harvey Nicks or San Lorenzo's for lunch. Then ready to slip down to Tramp's or Annabelle's in the evenings. But as I move into Belgravia, we move out to, of all places, Guildford. I wouldn't have minded, if it had been Holland Park; or even at a push, West Kensington. I could always have got a taxi to Harrods or somewhere. But Guildford? It's miles away from any form of civilisation.

JUDY: I don't know, they have a lovely theatre there.

KATE: That's true, darling... You don't know. What good is a theatre? I wanted some real life. Not just sit around watching some playwright's imaginary idea of life. And I wanted freedom. Now, after all those boring years with him... I've got it.

JUDY: If you were so unhappy, why didn't you leave earlier?

KATE: You don't think I was about to pass up the golden eggs, just because the goose wouldn't lay his wife. No, I just stuck it out. Night after night, scheming how to do it. How to get the golden eggs without upsetting the goose. That's where your crossword comes in. I suppose. Without crossword puzzles, the occasional Bridge party and the odd game of Patience. God knows, lots of patience! He might have guessed that I was fed up with the arrangement.

JUDY: Poor you.

KATE: Not so poor, dear! Life had its little compensations. After his initial attempts at consummating the marriage failed, by way of apology, he would buy me expensive jewellery... And I'm talking expensive! *(waves her arm and shows off her jewellery)* Also, surreptitiously, every week, I would bank some of the house-keeping money. And every month or two, I'd talk about inflation. Then ask

11

for more! He must have thought Guildford was on its own monetary system.

JUDY: Did you say you wanted tea?

KATE: No, don't you have anything stronger?

JUDY: Let me see. There's some cream sherry, if I can find it.

KATE: Don't even think about it! It'll remind me of Charles.

JUDY: Charles, why?

KATE: Sweet in very small doses. But too much and it's sickening.

JUDY: You are terrible.

KATE: No at all. Looking back, I was the perfect wife. The house was always clean, his evening meal was cooked and ready. Mind you, that was all due to Mrs Shaw, the housekeeper. But I discovered her. When he did eventually arrive home from work, like a good little girl, I was always there to pour his sweet sticky sherry. Before settling down to yet another dull dinner and an early night... At least the housekeeper could go to her room and get a good night's sleep. But I was the one who had to lie there with him snoring all night. Instead of sleeping, I ended up praying. *(JUDY looks surprised)* Praying... One night, he would wake, turn toward me and finally be able to get it up!

JUDY: *(embarrassed)* Kate, you always bring it down to sex!

KATE: *(smiles)* As you know, Charles wasn't particularly attractive. Yet, lying next to him, night after night, I actually began to wish that he would touch me. Not necessarily make love to me, but just hold me, so I knew, someone was there, that actually cared. Instead of someone with their back to me snoring and farting.

JUDY: But he must have loved you.

KATE: Loved? Oh, yes! He loved me. The same way he loved his art collection. We were both just decoration, to impress his business associates. Who, when they weren't ogling the expensive paintings on the wall, were ogling me. I was there to keep them amused with the odd witty bon mot and sophisticated quip.

JUDY: You're beginning to sound like Elsa Maxwell.

KATE: *(ignores the remark)* To begin with, it was a good arrangement. Almost a perfect one. Except for the lack of sex... And of course, the tediousness of it all. D'you know? His idea of fun was board games. I wouldn't have minded Backgammon. But Monopoly and Risk? The only risk for me was a nervous breakdown from boredom. In the end, I thought to myself, 'How could I have your lovely money, but have none of your dull company to go with it?'

JUDY: I'm sorry, it must have been very trying for you.

KATE: That was just it... In the end, I succeeded without having to try. All thanks to one of his old jackets.

JUDY: What does that have to do with it?

KATE: Everything! You see, I was going to donate it to a charity shop... And would you believe it?

JUDY: I might do if you told me.

KATE: While I was emptying out one of the pockets, what d'you think I found?

JUDY: I've no idea...

KATE: A Polaroid photograph of Charles.

JUDY: So?

KATE: He was in the bath... Completely naked!

JUDY: *(JUDY laughs)* Well, that's hardly surprising.

KATE: It was to me.

JUDY: Surely, you must have seen him in the bath before?

KATE: Yes, but not like this, wrapped in the arms of his personal assistant...

JUDY: *(seems shocked)* I'm so sorry.

KATE: That's when I realised the truth about him. More important-ly, that charity begins at home. At last, I had the bargaining power I needed to negotiate a very favourable settlement. However, I didn't bargain for him leaving me for his assistant. It seems, they were des-perate to set up home together, but terrified of a scandal.

JUDY: But I thought you left him?

KATE: Depends which way you look at it. I left that monotonous marriage and in return, he left me the house, a hefty sum of cash and a large chunk of his art collection. In return for... How should I put it? My discretion.

JUDY: That was very generous of him... That definitely shows Uncle Charles cared about you.

KATE: No dear, he was worried about me.

JUDY: That's what I mean... There we are, that proves it.

KATE: Not quite. He was worried I'd open my mouth. So instead, he bought my silence.

JUDY: Oh, I see. Was she younger than you?

KATE: *(doesn't look pleased)* You could say that.

JUDY: And was she pretty?

KATE: I wouldn't say pretty, exactly... But she certainly had balls!

JUDY: Sorry?

KATE: Darling, she was a he. It was a man.

JUDY: My goodness. Mother never mentioned he was like that?

KATE: *(interrupts)* She wouldn't, dear. Gay, outside of a jolly day, is well beyond her comprehension. Well, there you have it. Now you know why I gave up doing these. *(waves the paper)* They always remind me of those wasted years. *(A spring on the sofa suddenly bursts through and pricks her)* Ouch! *(jumps up and rubs her bottom)* Darling, you really must do something about this sofa. Like burn it!

JUDY: I'm sorry, I should have warned you about the broken spring. Let me help.

KATE: No, thanks! I can manage. *(puts her gloves back on)* Oh, look, my skirt! It's filthy. There's no excuse for this... it's so dusty. My dear, d'you really plan to live in this city?

JUDY: Of course, I do!

KATE: Then you must clean this place up... How could you possibly invite a man here?

JUDY: Be fair, I only moved in last night!

KATE: That's no excuse.

JUDY: Anyway, I don't know any men. *(heads off to the kitchen area)*

KATE: Then you really do need help, you're lucky I'm here.*(opens her compact and checks her make-up, but is interrupted by a ring at the door. Goes over and opens the door. ROGER stands in the doorway dressed in a battered tweed jacket, sweater and corduroy trousers)*

ROGER: Hello, I'm Roger. I live opposite. I just came to wish you welcome to our humble block of flats.

KATE: *(eyes ROGER up and down seductively)* That's very kind of you... Thank you.

ROGER: *(notices JUDY)* Oh, there's two of you?

JUDY: *(re-enters from the kitchen area)* No, this is my flat. I live alone. (*KATE acts snubbed*) Please, come in! I'm sorry about the mess.

ROGER: *(enters)* Don't worry, my place is still a mess and I've lived here six years.

JUDY: I hope it doesn't take me that long. By the way, this is Katherine, my mother's sister. *(Kate is touching up her make-up in her compact mirror)*

ROGER: So, you're her aunt?

KATE: Aunt? Oh, don't use that word. It's like this mirror. It reflects badly on my imagination.

ROGER: I'm sorry.

KATE: *(slams the compact shut)* Call me Kate, unless you prefer Kitty... Most men call me Kitty, *(winks at him)* But I suppose that's because underneath, I'm really just one big pussy.

ROGER: *(appears embarrassed).* I rather like Kate... It's short and succinct. *(Kate looks disappointed)*

JUDY: Yes, well this is turning into quite a busy morning, you're my second visitor. I wonder who's going to be my third?

KATE: If I were you, I'd settle for who's second. (*smiles at*

ROGER. JUDY pulls her away from him and whispers)

JUDY: Kate, stop it! You're undressing him with your eyes.

KATE: Oh, please! Just be grateful, I'm not doing it with my hands. *(walks back over to ROGER)*

JUDY: By the way, you never did tell me what you think of it?

KATE: *(flirts with ROGER)* Well...

ROGER: *(quickly speaks, to stop KATE vamping him)* Well, I think it's terrific! It's much bigger than mine.

KATE: How disappointing.

JUDY: *(glowers at KATE)* Give me your honest opinion?

KATE: *(Still staring at ROGER)* Beautiful, darling! And that chin is exquisite!

JUDY: About the flat!

KATE: *(slowly looks around)* Oh, well. It'll be alright, I suppose. It could be quite pleasant, it's just...

JUDY: It's just what? You don't like it, do you?

KATE: No, I do like it. But why choose such a dreary area? It's so far from Belgravia... Fulham, why Fulham?

JUDY: Money, of course! Even Fulham nearly broke the budget. This area is what they call up and coming. There are antique shops springing up everywhere.

KATE: Hmm, yes. Mainly owned by good-looking, young men who prefer needlework and bricklayers. It's so annoying, such a waste!

JUDY: Actually, it's not quite Fulham. We're on the border. The estate agent said that technically the bedroom is in Chelsea.

KATE: Yes! Well, I suppose, there's some hope then. Good, always answer your phone in the bedroom. Mind you, coming in, I did see a double-barrelled name on one of the bells. Check, if the owner has a signet ring and a new M.G. convertible. You could be in luck.

ROGER: Well, I think this flat is very nice.

KATE: Yes, I suppose it has potential... After a lot of work that is. *(sits in one of a the red leather chairs, then with her glove, tests for dust on the wing)* But you really must get yourself a housekeeper.

JUDY: I couldn't possibly afford one. I spent most of my trust money buying it.

KATE: Oh, please, leave being poor to the people living in Battersea. Remember, they have to cross that bridge to get to civilization.

JUDY: I'm serious. Dad even had to give me some extra furniture, so I could move in.

KATE: These chairs, I take it? They're nice enough. But a bit masculine.

JUDY: He bought them in Berlin, just after the war. I've really only room for one, but I can't choose which one, as their identical. So it would be a shame to break them up.

KATE: That's the least of your problems. To be honest, I just can't see the benefits of a colonel's daughter living in Fulham.

JUDY: Well, it couldn't be more dreary than Aldershot.

KATE: Yes, well... I won't argue with that.

ROGER: At least in Fulham, the rates are low.

KATE: The rates? *(looks at the dirt)* It's how high the mice are that worries me. In this area, knee deep, I should think.

ROGER: I must say, I like all animals, even rats.

KATE: That is encouraging. D'you like cougars?

ROGER: Sorry?

KATE: *(disappointed)* Forget it, darling. *(looks of at JUDY)* Now, that you're living in the fleshpots of London, what are you going to do with yourself... or shouldn't I ask?

JUDY: I'm hoping to get into a drama school. In fact, I have an audition for RADA in two weeks.

KATE: The Royal Academy, no less? I am impressed.

JUDY: Yes, well... It doesn't mean I'll get in. It's all a bit nerve-racking really.

ROGER: Well, they do say it's not easy in the theatre.

JUDY: You're telling me, as well as act, I have to sing something.

KATE: *(sarcastically)* How about a little Noel Coward? Something like, 'Don't put your daughter on the stage?' That would be perfect.

JUDY: *(ignores her suggestion)* I also have to recite some Shakespeare, as well as something from Oscar Wilde.

KATE: That's easy enough, dear. Do *Lady Bracknell*.. You know? The aunt, in that one about a child found on a train in a suitcase... Or was it a handbag?

ROGER: You mean, *The Importance of Being Earnest*?

JUDY: No, she's far too old.

KATE Well, at least, it stretches your age capabilities. I've been doing it for years... *(to herself)* in reverse. Okay, so what will you do?

JUDY: For a start, I'm not going to do anything from contemporary plays. Instead, I intend to recite the whole of Oscar Wilde's, T*he Ballad of Reading Gaol!*

KATE: I wouldn't, if I were you. That poem does go on forever. They'll be asleep before you finish.

JUDY: At least they'll be impressed that I managed to learn it.

KATE: If they are still awake by then.

JUDY: *(tuts)* It's a beautiful poem...

'He did not wear his scarlet coat,
For blood and wine are red,
(KATE looks to the heavens)
'And blood and wine were on his hands'...

KATE: Lovely, dear...

JUDY: *'When they found him with the dead'* ...

KATE: *'The poor dead woman whom he loved,*
And murdered in her bed.' Yes dear, that's bound to cheer them up!

ROGER: *(looks at JUDY)* Well, I agree. It's a marvellous poem. And, if I may say so, I think you'll be a wonderful addition to the theatre.

KATE: *(glowers at ROGER)* Well, so much for drama school. Darling, I think you'll have enough drama getting this place together. And as I said, you're going to need some help.

JUDY: I know, but I've hardly two brass farthings to rub together.

KATE: Then, obviously, you can't afford a proper housekeeper as such. So, get a char in.

JUDY: Char?

KATE: Charwoman... A Mrs Mop.... You know, a daily.. Or whatever they are called these days.

JUDY: A cleaner.

ROGER: Your aunt is right. If you get a domestic just to do the cleaning, then she's bound to be much cheaper.

KATE: Mind you, she won't cook or anything, but she'll certainly get this place straight. *(turns her attention back to ROGER)* So tell me, what d'you do with yourself?

ROGER: I'm a doctor.

KATE: *(looks over at JUDY)* Oh, that's useful, having your own personal doctor on the doorstep. *(turns back to ROGER)* What sort of doctor are you? I hope not one of these homoeopathic ones? I couldn't bear sipping green tea to cure my hangovers. I'd rather take my chances with a Buck's Fizz.

ROGER: I totaly agree... And to answer your question, I'm a gynaecologist.

KATE: It gets better! With this young cousin of mine, all alone with her bedroom on the edges of Chelsea, she may well be in need of your services...

JUDY: Kate, really!

KATE: You don't realise what all these arty types around here are like. *(JUDY'S embarrassed)* It's true, darling. You're not in Aldershot now.

JUDY: I do know that, auntie.

KATE: Don't keep broadcasting that fact, darling. Cousin sounds so much nicer. *(looks in her compact mirror)* And nearer the truth.

JUDY: *(smiles)* Well, I'm not a child any more. I am well over twenty one.

KATE: Not well over, darling... Don't age me too soon. If you are as old as you think you are... where does that leave me? Don't answer that!

JUDY: Oh, you'll never age. You never have.

KATE: Darling child, you always say the right thing. And sweetly enough, you mean it... I think?

ROGER: Well, if you ever get a bit lonely, I can always get seats to a concert, or an opera.

JUDY: Thank you, that's very sweet. Maybe, once I get things straightened out here. Either way, I certainly don't intend to be lonely. Who knows? I might find a boyfriend!

ROGER: *(Smiles)* Splendid idea!

JUDY: Someone nearer my own age.

KATE: Oops! My dear, *(looks at ROGER)* in Aldershot, she wouldn't say boo to a goose.

JUDY: That's because there weren't any... It was just a garrison town, full of soldiers.

KATE: Lucky you. I love a man in uniform. *(looks at her watch)* Now, I really must go. I'm late for my massage. My masseur is a hunky Italian who can't keep his hands off me... *(chuckles)* But then that's what I pay him for. Now, remember to get that cleaner.

JUDY: But where do I get one?

KATE: Fortnum & Mason...

JUDY: Really? Which department?

KATE: Don't be ridiculous! *(Looks at ROGER again)* Where does she get one? Where do you normally get one? The Lady Magazine of course.

ROGER: Better still, place an ad in the local newsagent's window.

KATE: Clever you, that's not such a bad idea. Anyone from there is bound to be cheaper.

ROGER: Also, they are more likely to be a local, so no excuses if she's late for work!

KATE: Yes, so do that! Now I really must go. I'm very late. Oh, look at the state of me. This St Laurent number cost a fortune! Next time I must remember to wear overalls, not haute couture.

JUDY: *(smiles and gives KATE a hug)* Thanks for coming... D'you really think it'll be alright?

KATE: What? *(walks towards the front door, still trying to brush off the dust)* Yes, I'll get it dry cleaned.

JUDY: I mean the flat.

KATE: Darling angel! I'm sure, the next time I pop in, it's going to look magic. *(To herself)* If you can find a magician, that is.

ROGER: *(As KATE opens the door, ROGER goes over to her)* You forgot your handbag. *(hands it to her)*

KATE:*(pecks him on the cheek)* What a sweetheart... These days, men usually try to steal it... I've even toyed with the idea of keeping a brick in it for safety. Well, darlings, see you very soon. *(again Pecks ROGER on the cheek)* Take good care of him, Judy... I think you stumbled across a treasure with this one. *(Again KATE pecks ROGER on the cheek)* Now, place that ad before the shop closes. Bye, darlings! *(exits and closes the door)*

ROGER: She's quite a woman, your aunt.

JUDY: She certainly is.

ROGER: I can see you're very close.

JUDY: No, not really. When I lived at home, I only ever saw her over Christmas, or some special family get together. But I do like her, she's so full of life and certainly the nearest thing to glamour I've ever seen. It's thanks to her, I decided to move to London and find out what living in the real world is all about.

ROGER: I'm glad you did.

JUDY: Yes, well, I'd better write out this ad. I couldn't bear it, if this place wasn't straight for her next visit.

ROGER: Have you got a card? Or an envelope will do.

JUDY: There must be one here somewhere. *(looks around)* How about the back of this card for a plumber?

ROGER: *(takes out a pen from his top pocket)* Perfect. Now let's see... What shall we put? 'Wanted hard-working cleaner, two hours a day, £3.10 shillings an hour.'

JUDY: That's not right.

ROGER: Why?

JUDY: Shillings and old pennies went out of circulation with decimalisation, remember?

ROGER: Of course, how stupid of me...

JUDY: *(chuckles)* It's been over two years now...

ROGER: Even so, I still can't get my head around it. Also, it seems everything is more expensive, as a result.

JUDY: Yes, prices do seem to have gone up.

ROGER: What I meant was, '£3.50 new pence an hour.'

JUDY: I can't afford that, especially two hours a day.

ROGER: Then what about 'conscientious cleaner required, £3.50 new pence an hour, for one hour a day?'

JUDY: That's better, but to clean this place up, it's going to take more than an hour a day.

ROGER: Well then, when she arrives, if you get on after the first couple of days, ask her to stay longer. *(writes out the card and hands it to JUDY)* Hey, presto! Voila, Madame!

JUDY: Lovely, thank you! Now, I'd better go and get it in the window before the shop closes.

ROGER: Before you shoot off... I was serious about the concerts. I really would appreciate a bit of company.

JUDY: Yes, that would be nice. But I have to get this place straight first.

ROGER: I do promise, it's just an invitation to listen to music... nothing else.

JUDY: Yes, I'd love to sometime. Now, I really must go and see to this ad.

ROGER: Be careful.

JUDY: Careful?

ROGER: Well, just make sure you don't get a cleaner, like the one that worked for my aunt.

JUDY: Why? Was she useless?

ROGER: On the contrary! But after the first week, she was picked up by the police for the attempted kidnapping of their sixth-month old baby.

JUDY: That's terrible. Well, luckily, I don't have children. Even so, I'll interview her thoroughly, I promise.

ROGER: Tomorrow?

JUDY: I doubt I'll get a response that quickly.

ROGER: No, to come to a concert with me. Or am I being too pushy?

JUDY: Well, it is a bit sudden... But then why not? I don't have any prior gilt-edged invitations... Okay, you're on. What time?

ROGER: Seven?

JUDY: Yes, seven is fine. *(ROGER opens the flat door)*

ROGER: *(Smiles)* Seven it is then! *(JUDY politely smiles at ROGER and closes the door. We hear piano music - 'These foolish things')*

Fade.

END OF SCENE I

ACT I SCENE II

Flat in semi-darkness, daylight peeping through the curtains. JUDY is asleep. The telephone is ringing. As JUDY wakes, she fumbles around looking for the phone. At the same time, the alarm on the radio starts buzzing.

JUDY: Hello, hello? *(drops the phone and picks it up again)* Sorry, please, can you speak up? This is a new line, there's a terrible buzzing. Can you hear it at your end? *(taps the phone on the floor, before realising it's the alarm and switches it off)* Hello, are you still there? Oh, hold on! Yes, I think this is Fulham 0921. Sorry, who is this? Ad, what ad? *(thinks for a moment)* Oh yes, for the cleaning job! When could you come? This afternoon... Great! Or this morning? *(seems surprised)* Well... Yes, I suppose you're right - sooner the better. Okay, see you soon. *(As she replaces the phone, it begins to ring again)* Hello? Oh, yes of course, my address. 5... Sorry, 3. Albert Mansions... 294 Fulham Road. That's right, SW10. My name? Hamilton, Judith Hamilton. Wonderful, bye. *(replaces the receiver and leaps out of bed)* Great! *(switches on the radio, seventies music plays. She quickly begins tidying up, by moving plates and glasses, which in her panic, only end up back in the same place. The intercom goes, so JUDY runs over to the door and pushes the buzzer. She then scampers back to the kitchen area, puts on the kettle, sniffs a half empty bottle of milk. prepares two mugs ready for tea. As she does, the post drops through the letterbox onto the floor. JUDY goes to the front door to collect it. As she bends down to pick it up, the door-bell rings, which startles her, causing her to hit her head on the broken letterbox cover. Rubbing her head she opens the door. JUDY looks stunned and drops the mail. MARK enters on roller skates, directly to centre-stage. He is wearing red satin shorts, a T-shirt that's too tight, with the motto 'Homme' on the front. He has bleached hair, and is wearing make-up. MARK is also wearing earphones attached to a portable cassette player attached to his belt. He is clutching a small leather grip bag. MARK then does an elaborate spin before he switches off his cassette)*

MARK: Honey, what a rare treat! I haven't seen dust like this since I cleaned the vicar's knickers! *(Eyes to heaven)* Ooh, what a thought. Hello, I'm Mark... Don't bother to kneel. *(JUDY seems horrified and is frozen to the spot. MARK skates back to the door, closes it, gently takes her hand and leads her to the sofa and sits her down)*

JUDY: Ouch! *(jumps up and rubs her bottom)*

MARK: I take it you're Judith? I'm Mark... Your new cleaner! *(JUDY appears to stiil be in shock. MARK puts a hand on her shoulder and gently pushes her back down)*

JUDY: Ouch!

MARK: Surely, I'm not that painful to look at.

JUDY: *(guides her bottom away from the protruding spring, and nervously answers)* Oh no, it's not you. It's just, I've got a loose spring.

MARK: So have I dear, but that never stopped me. *(The kettle whistles)* Oh, cheeky! Where do you keep your tea? *(picks up some empty glasses and skates over to the kitchen area, puts them down and opens a cupboard)*

JUDY: It should be...

MARK: Don't worry, I'll sniff it out. Now, what do we have in here? *(waves two tea bags before putting them in the mugs to make the tea)* And there was I thinking you were more of a sophisticated, Earl Grey and bone china teapot type? But what are you? A simple mugs and tea bags girl?

JUDY: That's all my corner shop stocks I'm afraid.

MARK: No problem. I'm a dab hand with a supermarket trolley, positively dangerous.

JUDY: Look, I'm not meaning to be rude, but I've got a bit of a headache coming on.

MARK: I have that effect on most people.

JUDY: No, it's not you. It's just that I banged my head on the mailbox cover, it's broken...

MARK: No problem. I'll soon fix that for you.

JUDY: I'm sorry, but you didn't tell me your name?

MARK: Didn't I? I'm Mark.

MARK: *(skates over to JUDY and hands her a mug of tea. (Before putting his mug down, he looks at the coffee table)* Ooh, the dust on here. *(hands JUDY his mug and skates back to the kitchen area. He opens a cupboard under the sink and brings out a tin of spray polish and a duster, then skates back to the table)* Quentin would be proud of you...

JUDY: Quentin?

MARK: Quentin Crisp. Surely, you've heard of him?

JUDY: I don't think so?

MARK: You're not serious? You've never heard of Quentin Crisp? He wrote that book, *The Naked Civil Servant.*

JUDY: No.

MARK: *(talks, as he begins dusting the coffee table and then the side tables)* Well, Quentin Crisp equals dust! It was Quentin who made the discovery that, if you don't do any dusting. After four years, the dust doesn't get any thicker... It just stays the same. It's known as Crisp's Law!

JUDY: I can't believe that.

MARK: In that case, I'll call back again in four years, and you can see for yourself if it works! *(JUDY puts the mugs back down on the coffee table)* Well, I'm off! *(MARK skates towards the door but JUDY doesn't react)* Bye! *(MARK still gets no response. So he skates back to the coffee table, picks up his mug and downs his tea in one)* Thanks for the tea. *(JUDY still seems to be distracted)* I'll see myself out. *(MARK skates back to the kitchen and washes up his mug. He hesitates, before skating back to the coffee table to pick up his bag)* Drink your tea, it's not poisoned. *(MARK then skates to the door)*

JUDY: *(as if talking to herself)* Oh, don't go.

MARK: *(doesn't need to be told twice and immediately skates back to JUDY)* Not if you don't want me to.

JUDY: Well, to be honest, you're not quite what I was expecting.

MARK: That's just what my mother said at my birth. *(JUDY still seems disoriented)* You alright? You did say to come round as soon as I could. So I put on me skates, grabbed me handbag and here I am. *(JUDY doesn't react)* You seem a bit dazed? It must be that knock on the head.

JUDY: No, it's not that. I'm sorry, if I come across that way. It's just...

33

MARK: It's just that you've never met someone like me before?

JUDY: Without appearing to be rude. No I haven't. *(MARK looks disappointed, picks up his bag and skates to the door. As he opens it, JUDY Looks around at what he has already managed to clean)* Look... Oh, why not? Come back. Yes, yes... let's give it a go.

MARK: You mean, you're taking me on?

JUDY: Yes, I suppose I am... But only for a trial period to see how we get on... Say a week or maybe two?

MARK: *(closes the door and skates back over to JUDY)* Don't you worry, we'll get on famously... Now let's get down to business.

JUDY: Business?

MARK: The business we spoke about on the blower. *(looks to the heavens)* Here we go again. Now Judy, may I call you Judy, or d'you prefer, I call you Ms, or Mrs Hamilton?

JUDY: It's Miss... and Judy is fine.

MARK: After Miss Garland herself, eh? *(impersonates Judy Garland, as he sings a couple of bars of 'The Man Who Got Away')* The road gets rougher, lonelier and tougher, and all because of the man who got away.' *(JUDY seems amused by his singing)* Ooh, I do like to identify with all her torment, don't you?

JUDY: *(grins)* I hardly think so. But I loved her in the 'Wizard of Oz'.

MARK: Yes, but I don't want to know where the rainbow really ends, do you?

JUDY: It'll be somewhere lovely, I'm sure.

MARK: *(to himself)* Wish I could be that certain. *(turns to JUDY)* Look, I know I may not be quite what you're looking for. But I do have me compensations. I'm not married or anything, so I'm what you might call, footloose and fancy free. Very flexible... *(winks)* With me hours that is.

JUDY: I see! Well, that's good.

MARK: And I have no other ties, so I can start immediately. *(looks around)* And as it so happens, I'm also a dab hand at decorating!

JUDY: Decorating?

MARK: Well, look at that wall, *(points to the grubby paintwork)* it's going to need a lick of something. I'm not a professional mind, but I do have a hidden talent for splashing the odd tin of paint around. And let's be honest, whatever bright colour I might choose to adorn these walls with can only be an improvement. I've seen a better shade of nicotine on a chain smoker's teeth. *(JUDY grimaces)* I know, how about a bright bold red? Not that orangey red, but a real red. Like a pillar box. It'll match those chairs.

JUDY: *(doesn't seem to be enthused)* I don't think so.

MARK: Then how about a subtle yellow? Now that really will cheer things up. Make the place feel permanently sunny.

JUDY: That sounds better

MARK: And maybe pale blue curtains and a blue cover on the sofa. Yes, a pale blue would compliment the yellow walls. Leave it to me. By the time I've finished, I wouldn't be surprised if *House and Garden* Magazine doesn't include it in their summer edition.

JUDY: You're joking?

MARK: How did you guess? Face reality, there's only so much I can do... *(To himself)* Without a bulldozer!

JUDY: I heard that! Sorry, it all sounds lovely, but I can't afford to decorate. At the moment, I just need a cleaner.

MARK: A cleaner you have, madam... me! A decorator you won't be needing. Because I'm prepared to offer my artistic talents. Free of charge, as a sort of thank you for taking me on.

JUDY: No, I don't think...

MARK: That's right, don't think! No buts and no thinking. *(JUDY looks surprised)* Look, I know on first meeting, I may appear a wee bit overpowering... But that's just my manner. You may not believe it, but I promise you, I'm really quite shy underneath. Come on... Just give me a chance to prove myself. That's all I ask.

JUDY: To be honest, the more I think about it, I'm really not sure...

MARK: Please, just for a trial period. I'll start first thing tomorrow morning. Then, if you are not satisfied with my work, I'll go. What have you got to lose?

JUDY: Well...

MARK: Well, nothing is the answer. Besides, I am fifty pence cheaper than anyone else. And remember, I'll be chucking in my decorating skills for free. It's a no - brainer. For you, it's a win-win. *(JUDY still seems unsure)* So it's a deal, yes? Go go on, say yes! Give it a go. *(MARK holds out his hand, JUDY pauses and then slowly puts out her hand)*

JUDY: Alright... I suppose. Okay, it's a deal! But only for a week or two. See how we get on. *(They shake hands)*

MARK: Done! *(MARK skates over to the front door and opens it)* See you tomorrow then. Oh, and I'll pick up some posh magazines to get some decorating ideas. *(MARK exits. JUDY goes to the door, opens it and calls after him)*

JUDY: But Mark, I don't have your number... How do I get hold of you?

MARK: *(V.O.)* That's right. You don't have to, I'll just appear... Like magic!

JUDY: But I haven't even got your address.

MARK: *(V.O.)* You don't need it... It's your place I'm cleaning remember... See you tomorrow. *(JUDY closes the door and shrugs)*

BLACKOUT
END OF SCENE II

ACT ONE

SCENE III

*Lights up. Three weeks later. The 1970's song 'Simple Simon Says'
is playing on the radio. MARK is alone in the apartment, which is
almost transformed. MARK is wearing an apron, T-shirt, knee-high
white socks, trainers and tight denim shorts. He is also wearing yellow rubber gloves. In time to the music, MARK is hoovering the car-
pet and putting the final touches of paint onto the walls with a brush.
As he pushes the paint brush upward, he pushes the vacuum cleaner
outward. As he brings the brush down, he pulls the vacuum cleaner
inward. The phone rings, he switches off the vacuum cleaner, rests
the brush, turns down the radio and answers it.*

MARK: *(In a camp French accent)* Allo... Non Madame, I am
afraid she is not 'ere... She is auditioning for ze part of ze French
Maid... zat's right. I do? No, I am not French. *(drops French accent
and switches to cockney)* Nah sorry, I'm from Sarf London. I've
just been 'elping 'er wiv 'er accent. I'm 'er new cleaner. Yes, dat's
right... Mark. Yes luv, I'm male. What d'you mean 'I don't sound
it'? *(drops his cockney accent)* If you've quite finished, I have work
to do. She should be back soon. Who shall I say called? katherine?
Is that a Miss or a Mr? *(The phone goes dead. MARK looks at it for*

38

a moment and replaces the receiver) Obviously a madam, a right madam. *(MARK switches the radio back on, which is now playing 'Day Dreamer' sung by David Cassidy, MARK picks up his paintbrush and goes back to hoovering, whilst painting at the same time)*

JUDY: *(JUDY enters and looks around)* Amazing... Mark, you really are a genius. *(realising that MARK can't hear, switches off the radio and instead taps him)* I said...

MARK: *(Mark is startled and turns off the vacuum)* What did you do that for? You could have given me a heart attack! Never creep up on me again.

JUDY: I'm sorry. I didn't mean to. I did shout, but you didn't hear me. *(upset by his reaction)* I only wanted to thank you. In just a few weeks, you've transformed the place... It's a miracle.

MARK: *(composes himself)* Well, not quite. But it will be once I get some more paint on that other wall. Then I'll cover that moth-eaten sofa, so it matches the new curtains.

JUDY: *(looks at the curtains)* Goodness knows what they'd have cost... new. Not to mention, what I would have had to pay for all this decorating.

MARK: *(MARK pulls out a loose sofa cover from a bag and drapes it over himself)* Not bad is it, dear? *(JUDY doesn't react)* Well, if you hate it, you'll love the price! It cost less than what you would pay for a new bra. It's from a charity shop.

JUDY: Looks lovely. *(JUDY looks at it and feels the material)*

MARK: It was in their half price sale. In fact, it was less than half price. Five quid!

JUDY: Five pounds?

MARK: It's originally from Peter Jones.

JUDY: That is ridiculous. Why so cheap?

MARK: I took the price tag off a grubby looking brassier and swapped them over. *(MARK throws it over the sofa)* Pull that end, will you, dear? *(JUDY takes one end and they begin to fit it over the sofa)*

JUDY: Hold on, you didn't really swap the price tags?

MARK: Why not?

JUDY: That's not just stealing... It's worse!

MARK: No, it's not! After all, I did pay for it. Just not the silly price they were asking.

JUDY: But it was a charity shop?

MARK: No, it's more like a junk shop really. *(MARK goes to one end of the sofa and pulls the cover tight and begins to tuck it in)* It's perfect... Look at it. It fits like a glove.

JUDY: Yes, I suppose it does. But it's still...

MARK: *(interrupts)* Stop fussing. *(MARK prods the sofa)* And see, and no nasty spring sticking out either. I fixed it. Come on, now sit down and try it. *(they both sit down)* Look! See, it matches the curtains from that other charity shop?

JUDY: Yes, it does... But it's still stealing.

MARK: It's not stealing. It's just another way of haggling, without having to haggle. Anyway, at the price they were asking, I could have bought the shop.

JUDY: Either way, it's disgraceful. How much was the real price?

MARK: Twenty five quid. Come on, just enjoy them, dear. There's no harm done. I promise, they were perfectly happy with what I gave them.

JUDY: How much did you really give them?

MARK: A fiver!

JUDY: What? But it's beautiful! Well, then you'll have to return it... It's worth much more.

MARK: No, it's second hand and worth what I'm willing to pay.

JUDY: *(picks up her purse)* Right then, here is your five pounds back. Tomorrow, I'll give you the other twenty pounds to give back to them. *(gives MARK the five pounds)* It is still a huge bargain. *(MARK looks sheepish)* You really are incorrigible!

MARK: I know, it's one of my many charms. Now come on, tell me about the audition?
JUDY: Not sure, but fingers crossed. I should know in a few weeks, in time for next term. To be honest, I found them a little bit snooty.

MARK: Snooty? That reminds me, someone rang for you. It was a woman... Katherine? I think.

JUDY: My aunt. What did she say?

MARK: Nothing, apart from insisting I was a female.

JUDY: What? But why? *(laughs)* Oh, Mark, I'm sorry, but on the phone you could easily be... When we first spoke, you even had me fooled.

MARK: Charming, I must say. Well, she sounded like a real cow!

JUDY: *(looks to the heavens and tuts)* I'm off to the loo.

MARK: Okay, I'll put the kettle on and make us a brew. *(JUDY goes into the bathroom, which can be seen upstage right, and closes the door. MARK goes to the kitchen area to make tea. The doorbell rings)* Judy, it's the door. *(MARK gets no reply)* Judy! Door, dear! *(MARK still doesn't get an answer, so he goes over and opens the door with a grand gesture)* Good morning, Madame.

KATE: Madame? But I'm not married!

MARK: *(to himself)* Why is that's no surprise. *(breaks into song in a German accent from the musical Cabaret)* Willkommen! Beinvenue! Welcome! Im Cabaret, au cabaret, to cabaret... Welcome!

KATE: *(Looks disgusted and brushes past him)* Where is she? Where is Miss Hamilton?

MARK: I'm afraid the star of our little cabaret is in the bathroom. But don't fret. As I'm doubling for the butler, may I offer you some tea Madame?

KATE: You must be the pansy I spoke to on the phone.

MARK: But you haven't answered my question. *(walks toward KATE with an exaggerated camp walk)* May I offer you some tea, Madame?

KATE: You can offer me nothing. *(continues the camp walk toward the kitchen and prepares the tea)* Disgusting!

MARK: But you haven't even tried it.

KATE: Are you really her domestic? Or is this a practical joke?

MARK: No joke. I am Judy's new cleaner.

KATE: It that what you are? Then remember, she is Miss Hamilton to you. You're being a little over familiar for an employee. Especially for a domestic.

MARK: Then you're not very observant. *(gestures to the room)* I'm also her decorator, interior designer... Oh, and her friend.

KATE: Friend? You're fooling yourself there, ducky. If she's paying you money, you'll find, like any other servant, you're just an employee.

MARK: *(smirks)* Really?

KATE: It can't be more than a month since I was last here. You certainly have gotten your feet under the table quick enough. You are a fast operator, I'll give you that.

MARK: I'll take that as a compliment.

KATE: Poor girl, she's always been gullible, not to mention naive. *(goes to the bathroom door and calls)* Judy! How long is she going to be in there? I can't wait around all day. Judy! What is she doing in there?

MARK: *(puts two mugs of tea on the coffee table)* She's probably taking a shower.

KATE: *(Glowers at MARK)* I didn't ask you.

MARK: You just did!

KATE: I was asking myself. Look, if you intend staying on in Miss Hamilton's employ, don't speak unless you are spoken to. I've had my fill of your kind!

MARK: Well, lucky you.

KATE: Oh, please! Don't flatter yourself. I have no end of suitors falling at my feet.

MARK: Yes, I've heard there's been a shortage of Zimmer frames lately. *(walks over to the kitchen)*

JUDY: *(enters from the bathroom in her dressing gown. She is brushing her hair)* Kate, what a lovely surprise! *(gives her a kiss)* How long have you been here? *(goes over to the coffee table and picks up her tea)*

KATE: Don't ask, it seems like eternity. By the way, the door to the main entrance was wide open...

JUDY: It's probably the latch, it's a bit loose. I'll talk to the managing agents.

KATE: Anyone could have walked in!

MARK: *(to himself)* Seems they already have.

KATE: I broke my shopping trip to come here, to see if you managed to find a charwoman. And what do I find? Him! Or should I say it? *(gestures toward MARK)*

MARK: It is no more I than you are me, Madame.

KATE: Stop calling me Madame!

MARK: Oh, please, keep your wig on.

KATE: You see that, Judy? Since I arrived, nothing but insults. You should get rid of him...

JUDY: Mark, don't be so rude.

MARK: She started it! She called me pansy. Now she's saying I'm odd. I'm not odd, am I?

JUDY: Of course you're not.

KATE: Don't be so blind. Of course he is. Just look at him. *(points at MARK'S outfit)* What did he do, get dressed in the dark?

JUDY: Kate, for goodness sake, stop it.

KATE: Oops! *(Sarcastically)* If that's how you feel... I wouldn't dream of upsetting this domestic bliss.

JUDY: Oh, really...

KATE: Take it from me, you'd best keep your eye on him. There's something very fishy going on.

JUDY: How can you say that? He's been an absolute godsend!

KATE: I'm sure God had nothing to do with it... Quite the opposite I should think.. *(gestures toward the floor)*

JUDY: Look around, you can't deny it. Mark's worked a miracle on this place.

KATE: Oh, please... Just listen to yourself.

MARK: *(Doorbell rings)* I'll get it.

KATE: *(to MARK)* No, you stay where you are, I'll get it.

JUDY: Well, at least, one of you get it, I have to change. *(exits to the bedroom, as MARK picks up the mugs and goes over to the kitchen area)*

KATE: With any luck, it might be someone normal. *(opens the front door)* And so it is. Hello, we've met before. Come in. *(ROGER enters puffing on a pipe)* What is that dreadful smell?

ROGER: I'm so sorry, it must be this. *(looks at his pipe)* I'll put it out. *(walks over to a side table and bangs his pipe on an ashtray)*

KATE: No, it's not that. I love the aroma of pipe tobacco; it's like you Roger... Masculine! *(winks at ROGER)* No, this isn't an aroma... It's a stink! Please, light up again; it might help kill it. *(As KATE goes over to the kitchen, ROGER gets out his tobacco pouch, takes out some tobacco, then places the pouch on the table, next to where MARK has put his leather bag. ROGER loads his pipe, then picks up MARK'S bag and puts it into his pocket, leaving the pouch on the table. ROGER doesn't light his pipe)*

KATE: It's over here... It smells disgusting. *(JUDY enters from the bedroom)*

JUDY: Hi Roger... What's disgusting?

KATE: That is. *(points to Mark stirring a saucepan. MARK tastes the contents and then offers KATE a spoon to have a taste)*

MARK: Taste it!

KATE: *(brushes the spoon away)* Yuck! Sorry to disappoint you, but I'm not the suicidal type.

MARK: If only you were. Judy, you'd like some, wouldn't you?

JUDY: *(looks into the saucepan)* Well, it is a bit early in the day for custard. *(sniffs the contents)* She's right, there is a whiff of something and it's not custard.

MARK: Don't be daft, that's just the egg poaching. *(picks up a plate containing a bun with some ham on it. He takes the egg out of the frying pan and puts it on the ham, then pours the contents of the saucepan onto it)* And this certainly isn't custard, it's Hollandaise sauce! *(hands JUDY the plate)*

KATE: Brave girl, personally I wouldn't touch it!

JUDY: I'm sure it's lovely.

KATE: What on earth is it meant to be?

MARK: Eggs Benedict, of course! Probably a little adventurous for you. Best you keep practising laying them.

JUDY: *(sits on the sofa and begins to eat)* Kate, try it... mmmm, it's delicious. Mark, there is no end to your talents. Come on, try it! *(JUDY offers her a taste)*

KATE: *(looks disgusted)* No, thanks. You know me, I'm sensitive to poison! Anyway... I really have to be going. *(MARK sits down next to JUDY. KATE looks over at the Eggs Benedict)* Oh, look at it... It doesn't even marry with the sauce!

MARK: I'm not surprised! They've only just met! *(MARK and JUDY giggle)*

KATE: It's not normal, you know.

JUDY: What isn't?

KATE: Allowing him to sit next to you... As if he owns the place. After all, he's just your cleaner!

JUDY: No, that's not quite right. Mark's become much more than that.

KATE: Yes, I can see. *(scribbles something on a scrap of paper and hands it to JUDY)*

JUDY: *(reads it)* Nine, nine, nine? What's that for?

KATE: In case you need a stomach pump. More importantly, if you have any problems with him.

MARK: *(stands up)* What do you mean by that?

KATE: I don't think I have to spell it out. I'm sure, you know all too well what I mean.

JUDY: Come on, now stop this.

KATE: I'm serious, don't turn your back on this one... I don't trust him. I can't put my finger on it, but I will.

MARK: Maybe you should... *(holds his crotch)* ...Put your finger on it... It might take away your frustrations.

JUDY: *(Exasperated)* Oh please, both of you... Enough!

KATE: I wonder what you're really like, underneath all your vulgar gestures and cheap little guttersnipe one-liners?

MARK: Do us a favour, just straighten your wig and leave.

KATE: Now, there's a turn up for the books! The servant becoming the master. It's you who should leave... Preferably back to whatever asylum you escaped from.

JUDY: Mark you're being very rude, now stop it!

KATE: Exactly! About time, you put him back in his box.

MARK: *(Walks over to KATE and whispers)* Just piss off!

KATE: No chance! Just remember, you're a nothing in my book.

MARK: Then for your sake, I hope it's a very slim volume... Otherwise you might not live long enough to finish it.

KATE: Judy, did you hear that? He just threatened me.

JUDY: *(isn't paying attention)* What? Oh, now just stop it! And I mean both of you.

KATE: Well, you can hardly blame me for his bad behaviour.

ROGER: *(goes over to KATE)* Come on Kate, let's go.

JUDY: *(attempts to change the subject)* I must say, as usual, you're looking very elegant.

KATE: *(smiles as she touches her skirt)* Yes, I am, aren't I. But then for what this cost, I should do.

JUDY: But then you always do. Another Norman Hartnell?

KATE: No, dear.

JUDY: Hardy Amies?

KATE: Nope, it's not English.

JUDY: French? Then, it's either Coco Chanel... Or Yves St Laurent?

KATE: Wrong. again.. Pierre Cardin! But it is French...

What else would it be?

MARK: American.

KATE: American?

MARK: One Yank and it's off!

JUDY: *(KATE is not amused. JUDY tries not to giggle and so changes the subject)* Kate, Why don't you drop by again next week when this place is finally finished. I'm sure by then, everything will look very different.

KATE: This place might, but he certainly won't. He'll look exactly the same... Weird. And I mean in more ways than one.

JUDY: Oh, come now.

KATE: Roger, you're a normal man. Be honest, what do you make of him?

ROGER: Well I...

KATE: Don't you find him repulsive?

ROGER: Not at all.

KATE: Oh no, I couldn't bear it. Don't tell me you're one of them as well?

ROGER: What d'you mean?

KATE: What d'you think I mean? Just look at the way he's dressed...

(As KATE continues, MARK walks over to the one of the armchairs, sits down and hugs a cushion) Not to mention that dyed hair and the fact he's wearing make-up.

ROGER: I really think we should go.

KATE: You do surprise me. Just when things are getting interesting. Oh do look, he's pretending to be upset.

ROGER: Come on, let's leave.

KATE: You keep an eye on him for me, Roger. I'm intrigued to know what he's really up to.

MARK: *(seems upset)* You flatter me.

KATE: Not intentionally, I assure you. Just remember, I'm not gullible like she is.

MARK: Why are you so suspicious? You don't even know me.

KATE: Ah, but I intend to.

JUDY: This is going too far. Kate, I think you should leave.

KATE Well, well. I can see who's side you've taken.

JUDY: I haven't taken any sides.

KATE: Come on, you must admit it is strange, how in such a short time he's managed to worm his way into your confidence... Just like adding water, then poof! An instant friendship!

JUDY: It's me who's going to drama school, not you.

KATE: Yes, well, I'd better be off. I'd hate to be late for my masseur. After this, I'm definitely in need of a good rubdown.

ROGER: Yes, I should be off, too. Come on Kate, I'll walk you down.

JUDY: But Roger, you've hardly said one word.

ROGER: *(Looks at MARK and KATE)* To be fair, I haven't had much of a chance. I just wanted to know if you'd like to come to a concert. But as you're eating, I'll come back later.

JUDY: After all this, I've lost my appetite. Tell me, what is it?

ROGER: Mahler, at the Festival Hall. It's being conducted by Sir-George Solti no less.

JUDY: Yes, I'd like that very much. *(MARK seems disappointed, but quickly hides it)*

KATE: If you ask me, I prefer a good musical with a happy ending.

ROGER: I've taken a sabatical from work, so we could do that next week.

KATE: Good, then take her to that new one that's just opened...

ROGER: Which one's that?

KATE: The Rocky Horror Show...

JUDY: *(half heartedly)* Lovely.

KATE: *(looks over at MARK)* I'm surprised you didn't audition, it sounds like type casting, with that title.

JUDY: Oh, Kate honestly!

KATE: *(opens the door)* Well, goodbye, I do hope there's been no trouble on my account. *(giggles as she exits with ROGER)*

JUDY: Bye. *(JUDY walks over and closes the front door. Then goes over to the armchair to comfort MARK)* I'm really sorry about that. She really doesn't like you, does she?

MARK: Oh, just water off a duck's back dear! I have an aunt just like her... She can't stand me either.

JUDY: Really?

MARK: Yes, she has the same vicious tongue.

JUDY: Funny, it's the first time you've mentioned your family since you've been here.

MARK: There's been no reason to. You've never asked.

JUDY: I suppose I haven't... Well, I'm asking now.

MARK: What can I say? I suppose, they're just typically lower middle class, with high moral attitudes.

JUDY: Meaning?

MARK: Meaning, they can't handle what they refer to as my moral degeneracy.

JUDY: Really?

MARK: Yes, even the family dog can't stand me.

JUDY: Now you're making fun of me.

MARK: It's true! When I go home, our pet goldfish is the only one pleased to see me, but I put that down to his short memory span.

JUDY: *(chuckles)* Any brothers or sisters?

MARK: Neither...

JUDY: What about friends?

MARK: Not really...

JUDY: But everybody has friends...

MARK: Do they?

JUDY: Yes, well at least one person, they can call a friend...

MARK: *(Sarcastically)* Lucky them.

JUDY: Come on, you must have at least one, surely?

MARK: I did once... But that was a long time ago.

JUDY: Did this friend have a name?

MARK: Does it matter?

JUDY: Not if you don't want to tell me...

MARK: Matt...

JUDY: As in Matthew?

MARK: As in what else?.

JUDY: What happened to him?

MARK: I don't see him any more.

JUDY: Why not?

MARK: Wow, so many questions! As I said, it was a long time ago. It was just a childhood friendship... We were inseparable.

JUDY: So, what changed?

MARK: We grew up.

JUDY: Meaning?

MARK: As we did, we grew further apart.

JUDY: But why?

MARK: .We became very different people. Maybe I'll tell you one day. Anyway, let's not talk about him. Tell me more about your crazy aunt...

JUDY: *(laughs)* She's not crazy. I just think she sees you as competition.

MARK: Competition?

JUDY: With Roger.

MARK: What? But I would never... He's so ordinary, he abuses the privilege!

JUDY: Oh, he's nice.

MARK: All that back slapping and pipe smoking, it's not normal. It's him your aunt should be suspicious of, not me. *(stands up)*

JUDY: She's just overly protective, that's all. *(pats the sofa for him to sit down)* By the way, thank you.

MARK: For what?

JUDY: For everything. *(gestures toward the room)*

MARK: I should be thanking you. Most people, the moment they clapped eyes on me, would have asked me to leave. They would never have given me houseroom, let alone employ me. You gave me a chance... And I'm really grateful.

JUDY: To be fair, you didn't give me much say in the matter; you never allowed me to get a word in. *(laughs)* You were outrageous, turning up in roller skates of all things. I suppose, I was stunned into submission.

MARK: *(chuckles)* Yeah, well, you did seem a bit nervous.

JUDY: I certainly was. It was a big move coming to London. Apart from Kate, I didn't know anyone... Before you arrived, I felt very much alone...

MARK: I'm sorry.

JUDY: Don't be sorry, it's thanks to you, I don't anymore.

MARK: *(puts his arm around JUDY as she snuggles up to him)* It's funny, you know. People accuse me of being all kinds of things, things I'm not... Just because of the way I carry on.

JUDY: *(scoffs)* You'll be telling me next you like women...

MARK: I do.

JUDY: What? I would never have guessed.

MARK: I don't be silly. I mean, you know..? The way I like you...

JUDY: Which is?

MARK: Now that would be telling.

JUDY: Be serious.

MARK: You wouldn't like me if I were. You only put up with me, because I make you laugh...

JUDY: Rubbish! You're talking nonsense.

MARK: I'm not, I promise you. *(looks over at the red leather chairs)* Have you decided which one to keep?

JUDY: Sorry?

MARK: I could put some nice fabric on them... Make them blend in more?

JUDY What are you talking about?

MARK: The chairs, which one you getting rid of?

JUDY: Oh, I don't know, it just seems a shame to break them up.

MARK: I suppose, but you'll have to make a choice sooner or later.

JUDY: I know... Now come on, get back to what you were telling me about your family.

MARK: But I just told you.

JUDY: Okay, but why is it you never seem to want to talk about yourself?

MARK: I could say the same about you. You don't give much away.

JUDY: There's nothing much else to know. You've seen for yourself.

MARK: Only that you want to be an actress... That you were brought up in the countryside and that your father was in the military.

JUDY: Yes he was. My father was a colonel, but he's retired now. He was stationed in Germany after the war... Infact, I was born there.

MARK: He must be knocking on a bit by now then?

JUDY: Don't be so rude!

MARK: I'm only joking! So what's he like?

JUDY: He's lovely, both my parents are.

MARK: Any brothers or sisters?

JUDY: No, sadly.

MARK: Why was that sad?

JUDY: You really are a nosy parker!

MARK: Not at all. I'm just curious... It seems we were both the only child.

JUDY: In my case, my parents married relatively late in life. So they never dreamed they'd be able to have any children... I came as a pleasant surprise!

MARK: *(laughs)* I bet! Poor old things!

JUDY: You can stop that right now!

MARK: I'm only joking!

JUDY: Maybe, but it was no joke for my mother. She was over forty, when I was conceived. And against all the doctors advice, she still went ahead with the birth... She was in labour for hours. It certainlywasn't an easy birth.

MARK: I bet. *(sticks out his stomach and then pushes it with both hands and puffs and pats it)* Well, I'm am glad she managed it... Otherwise, I would never have met you.

JUDY: *(frowns)* Yes well, I think that's enough about my childhood.

MARK: But you've hardly told me anything...

JUDY: Because you keep larking about.

MARK: I'm sorry... *(pulls his stomach in, then noisily exhales)* So what was it like growing up?

JUDY: *(tuts)* I had a great childhood thank you. My parents having had me so late, I think they valued having a child that much more....

MARK: Yes, I suppose they would.

JUDY: We were a close-knit family. We still are. As a child, I suppose, you could say, I was cosseted. And in some ways, cut off from the rest of the world... But there we are.

MARK: You don't sound too happy about that

JUDY: It was only natural, them being that much older, that they wanted to spend as much time with me as they could. Before I grew up and went out into the world.

MARK: I can understand that...

JUDY: Don't get me wrong, I was very happy. Yet at times, it did get a bit lonely. But thankfully, things changed when I was sent off to boarding school.

MARK: Where did you go?

JUDY: An all girls school in Sussex... Rodean.

MARK: Yes, I've heard of it? Very posh! Jolly hockey sticks and all that!

JUDY: Yes, well, hockey and netball were never my thing. I hated sport, apart from swimming... Oh, and I was good at tennis. But like any sport, I do find it boring just to sit and watch.

MARK: Rodean wasn't for you then...

JUDY: Don't get me wrong! No, I loved it there. That's where I made some really good friends.

MARK: *(disappointed)* What happened to them?

JUDY: Oh, they're dotted around in different parts of the world now. Most of them are married with kids.

MARK: *(relieved)* So why aren't you?

JUDY: Is this a chat or an interrogation? You are getting very personal...

MARK: I'm just interested, that's all... You've never told me any of this before.

JUDY: You've never asked before.

MARK: So why didn't you get married?

JUDY: In Aldershot, there wasn't exactly a large selection of candidates. But now I'm in London... Who knows. Now enough of this. It's only fair that you start answering questions.

MARK: Such as?

JUDY: Why do you keep your address a secret?

MARK: What do you need it for?

JUDY: What if there were an emergency, and I needed to get in contact? Why all the cloak and dagger? The big mystery?

MARK: There's no mystery. It's just my landlady doesn't allow visitors. If you suddenly turned up, she'd probably throw me out. So what's the point in you having it? Unless of course you insist.

JUDY: No, but then what about a phone number? She can't object if I call surely?

MARK: Probably not, but she'd be shocked.

JUDY: By me ringing?

MARK: Of course.

JUDY: That's crazy, why would she be shocked?

MARK: Because she doesn't have a phone.

JUDY: Very funny.

MARK: It's true. So what else d'you want to know?

JUDY: Anything.

MARK: Anything?

JUDY: And everything. For starters, where do you come from?

MARK: Originally?

JUDY: Yes.

MARK: Bristol.

JUDY: I've been there. I have a cousin, lives in Clifton...

MARK: *(Surprised)* Really?

JUDY: It's a beautiful city.

MARK: Not where I was brought up... It's a real dump.

JUDY: Oh, I see. *(flustered)* Oh, dear, how dreadful.

MARK: Not really, it didn't bother me.

JUDY: Do they still live there?

MARK: Who?

JUDY: Your family...

MARK: My dad does.

JUDY: What's he like?

MARK: He's a fat, beer swigging bully, who can't stand the sight of me.

JUDY: Oh, dear... And your mother?

MARK: Quite the opposite, she was a sweet natured, timid creature... and very religious.

JUDY: Was?

MARK: She's dead.

JUDY: I'm sorry.

MARK: It's hardly your fault.

JUDY: Well, hopefully she didn't suffer.

MARK: She suffered alright... It was my father's bullying that drove her to an early grave. He as good as killed her.

JUDY: Oh, I'm so sorry.

MARK: There you go again...

JUDY: I don't know what else to say... It must have been horrible.

MARK: Yes, it was. That's probably why she turned to religion. I think it was her way of coping.

JUDY: He sounds like a monster. Did he hit her?

MARK: What d'you think? My father would often arrive home drunk, after the pubs had closed and hit her for no reason...

JUDY: He sounds absolutely ghastly...

MARK: Mind you, he'd always find some lame excuse to do it. Such as, if his dinner had gotten cold, or was over cooked, because he always arrived back so late.

JUDY: Did he ever hit you?

MARK: Put it this way, he never kissed me.

JUDY: What does that mean?

MARK: I learned how to handle him. *(laughs)* One day, he went too far. He called me a dirty little poof, so I hit him back. He never tried it again. From then on, just for fun, I used to be outrageous and camp around the house.

JUDY: *(Chuckles)* What did he make of that?

MARK: It freaked him out. He'd leave the room as soon as he saw me.

JUDY: Even so, it must have had an affect on you?

MARK: How d'you mean?

JUDY: Well, most people would have had a nervous breakdown or something. I know I would have...

MARK: No, nothing like that.

JUDY: You were lucky then.

MARK: Yes, I suppose I was compared to that mate of mine... He had it much worse.

JUDY: I can't imagine how?

MARK: His father didn't have to be drunk to hit him. He got sadistic pleasure out of it. You should have seen the bruises on him.

JUDY: What happened to him?

MARK: His father got away with it...

JUDY: I meant your friend. How is he?

MARK: Matt? It affected him very badly. He seemed to lose his confidence. I could hardly get him to leave his room. He was just no fun anymore,

JUDY: Poor boy.

MARK: In other ways, he was lucky.

JUDY: Lucky?

MARK: Unlike me, he grew up to become a really goodlooking bugger and strong with it. Can you believe it? He didn't settle for a six pack, he had an eight pack.

JUDY: Mmmm, he sounds like quite a hunk.

MARK: And what have I got? *(looks at his stomach)* A one pack that fits all.

JUDY: *(giggles)* Come off it, you're just fishing for compliments. There's nothing wrong with you that a little dieting wouldn't cure.

MARK: No, but he really is fit... He's also very hansome. You know the type, piecrcing blues eyes and thick dark hair.

JUDY: I do, that's very much my type.

MARK: Hey, stop that! Show some sympathy. Look what I got saddled with. Boring brown eyes and straggly blond... *(coughs)* ish hair...

JUDY: *(looks at him suspiciously)* Is that colour real?

MARK: Yes, of course! Why ask? *(to himself)* It went blond with grief.

JUDY: Really? Well, blond hair and those big brown eyes of yours, are very nice too... To be honest, I wouldn't throw you out of bed.

MARK: In that case, I'd better start making you apple-pie ones.

JUDY: *(laughs)* Oh, come off it. We did that in school. Folding the sheets back, just so the other girls couldn't get into bed... Don't even think about it!

MARK: Hmm, yes, I just might have to give it some serious thought.

JUDY: Now, getting back to this Mathew. Is he really that good looking? Or are you just just making it up?

MARK: Sadly, no... He is that good looking!

JUDY: Mmmm, he definitely sounds interesting.

MARK: Oh, please, that's the last thing he is.

JUDY: Why?

MARK: He used to be good fun, when we were younger... Before he became so bloody withdrawn.

JUDY: After what he went through, that's understandable.

MARK: I suppose. But he spent most of his time locked in his room...

JUDY: Doing what?

MARK: Reading, mainly... Always books about computers. He became a real computer nerd.

JUDY: Nice! Brains, as well as looks.

MARK: *(tuts and looks to the heavens)* Remind me? How did he manage to creep back into the conversation?

JUDY: I asked if he was that good looking..

MARK: And I should have said he wasn't... That he was a really ugly bugger.

JUDY: Too late! So, while he was studying away and being productive, what were you doing?

MARK: I was out having a good time. Occasionally, I did manage to prize him out of his room, and drag him to a club to meet girls. But I gave up in the end.

JUDY: Why?

MARK: Don't get me wrong, he's as straight as a die, yet he can hardly bring himself to speak to girls.

JUDY: Aah, he sounds really sweet... He's probably just shy.

MARK: Oh, please! There's no denying they all fancied him, but after the first couple of dates, sure enough, they'd dump him.

JUDY: Wht? What did he do?

MARK: That's just it, nothing.

JUDY: There must have been a reason?

MARK: There was... They found him boring.

JUDY: That's sad...

MARK: I think it's funny. After all, it's his own fault.

JUDY: I mean, it's sad that you don't see him anymore.

MARK: Not really...

JUDY: But why? If you were such good friends?

MARK: Because he began to hate me... And I mean, really loathe me.

JUDY: That doesn't make any sense. You said you were great friends.

MARK: Don't you get it? Matthew, the clever, straight, introverted computer nerd, having to rely on me, the flamboyant, poofy exhibitionist to fix him up with girls?

JUDY: The poor boy.

MARK: Poor boy? It was his choice, to shut himself away in his room... And don't forget, it was me that prized him out of it.

JUDY: Yes, but...

MARK: Without me, he would never have gone to a nightclub. Let alone met girls. It's as simple as that.

JUDY: Maybe he was just lacked confidence.

MARK: But, as I say, we made a good team. His good looks... And my naturally gregarious personality, that got us into most places. That was, until he started having strange little mood swings.

JUDY: Meaning?

MARK: For no apparent reason, he would create an argument and get angry.

JUDY: Maybe he was more angry with himself.

MARK: But why?

JUDY: For being dependent on you... Would be my guess.

MARK: But as I say, we made such a good team.

JUDY: Yes, but he was still dependent on you. And nobody should be dependent on someone else for their happiness.

MARK: Well he certainly was. And there was no gratitude. Instead he accused me of ruining his life.

JUDY: How?

MARK: By being too outrageous... Embarrassing him in public. Me? Too outrageous... Can you imagine?

JUDY: Yes, I can easily.

MARK: Oh, thanks! Sounds like you two deserve each other!

JUDY: My guess is, he's just frustrated that he can't be more like you.

MARK: You mean camp?

JUDY: Extrovert.

MARK: Huh! I doubt that. We even had a blazing row about it. It nearly came to a fist fight...

JUDY: I can't imagine that...

MARK: Don't you worry I can stand up for myself. True, physically he was much stronger, but that didn't bother me. Not until he started screaming and shouting.

JUDY: Why?

MARK: I suppose, it was the fact, that he was usually such a quiet, person, that I found it unerving... Especially when he threatened to kill me.... That really was frightening.

JUDY: Oh, come on! In the heat of the moment, we all say silly things we don't mean.

MARK: No, he meant it, alright. You should have seen the look on his face; he was serious. That's the reason I moved to London... And now I've heard he's also moved up here.

JUDY: Really?

MARK: So perhaps, you'll now understand why I'm not eager to give out my address.

JUDY: I thought you said, it was because of your landlady.

MARK: That's right.

JUDY: Forgive me, Mark, but I'm having difficulty trying to work out what the truth is here? Your landlady? Or this Matthew?

MARK: You are going on a bit, dear... You're driving me to a cig-arette. *(goes to the table for his bag, finds ROGER'S pouch, picks it up, looks at it and puts it down)* Where's my bag? *(begins to look for his bag)* That's strange, where is it? I know I brought it with me. *(searches around)* Where is it?

JUDY: Stop looking for your bag, it's bound to be here somewhere... Or is this just an excuse not to answer my question?

MARK: I promise you, I'm not lying... Why would I? My landla-dy really doesn't allow visitors... And I'm certainly not taking any chances of Matt finding out where I live... Satisfied?

JUDY: Yes, but why all this cloak and dagger over a silly argument?

MARK: It was more than just a silly argument.

JUDY: Sounds like you're overreacting. I'm sure he didn't mean what he said...

MARK: He meant it alright... You should have seen him. No, he got very nasty.

JUDY: Well, you can't keep running away. You should just face up to him.... See him again. And, if he apologises, give him another chance. If he doesn't, then just draw a line under it all.
MARK: No way...

JUDY: If you ask me, life's too short... Especially, as you used to be such good friends.

MARK: Forget it, I've moved on and it's about time he did.... I don't want to be stuck down memory lane. Now, come on! Help me find my bag, then I must go... *(picks up his jacket and puts it on)*

JUDY: Where did you get that? It's fabulous.

MARK: You like it?

JUDY: I love it... It's a bit outrageous. But on you, it's perfect.

MARK: Not sure that's meant as a compliment?

JUDY: Of course it is. If only I had the nerve to wear things like that.

MARK: What do you mean 'nerve'?

JUDY: Well, not nerve exactly... I mean dare to wear.

MARK: You mean clothes you wouldn't be caught dead in?

JUDY: No! You know what I mean. The way you dress. You said it yourself. It's flamboyant... It's fun.

MARK: Now you're saying I'm a clown? Come on, be honest, spit it out! Don't you mean freak?

JUDY: What's gotten into you? No, I don't! Don't be so insecure. You're no more a freak than I am.

MARK: You're sweet, but I know what I am.

JUDY: Now, come on! Can I try it on?

MARK: *(Reluctantly)* If you really want to. *(takes off his jacket and JUDY tries it on)* It suits you. It really does... Keep it.

JUDY: Don't be silly, I couldn't do that.

MARK: Go on, keep it. I mean it.

JUDY: But, I couldn't possibly...

MARK: Now it's you being paranoid. Keep it. Please, I'd like that.

JUDY: But you can't afford to give things away, not on what you earn. Or should I say, thanks to me, what you don't earn? This must have cost a small fortune?

MARK: That's where you're wrong, it probably costs me more to wear it. *(JUDY takes off the jacket and goes to hand it back)* No, I said 'keep it'!

JUDY: If you're sure, then thank you... You know, it's funny really.

MARK: Me? Or the jacket?

JUDY: It's funny how in just a few weeks, you've become an integral part of my life. I'm not sure what I'd do if you left.

MARK: Why would I? Unless you fire me.

JUDY: I'd never do that!

MARK: That's a relief. Let's face it, no one else would employ me. Most people would want to burn my jackets, not wear them.

JUDY: *(laughs)* Oh, Mark! You do make me laugh...

MARK: Good. *(becomes serious)* Will you promise me something?

JUDY: What's that?

MARK: When I arrive in the mornings, if you can, try and always be here.

\JUDY: Why? What if I weren't?

MARK: It may sound silly, but just be here... That's all.

JUDY: I'm not sure what you mean?

MARK: Look, *(looks around the room)* this place is nearly finished.

JUDY: Yes, I know. And I can't thank you enough...

MARK: That's not what I meant. I mean very soon, I'll be here for just an hour or so in the mornings.

JUDY: But why?

MARK: Because, I'll just be your cleaner again.

JUDY: No, you won't... You'll always be more than that. You're my friend, my best friend.

MARK: Maybe, but it'll be only a matter of time before you meet someone.

JUDY: Meaning?

MARK: *(nods)* Things will change... You'll find a boyfriend.

JUDY: *(scoffs)* Boyfriend? Fat chance!

MARK: Maybe you're right... And I am probably just talking rubbish.

JUDY: Rubbish? What d'you mean rubbish? *(JUDY smiles)* I'm not that ugly!

MARK: No, of course you're not. *(MARK gently touches her cheek)*

JUDY: *(looks surprised)* Hold on. *(MARK withdraws his hand)* If I did meet someone, are you saying you'd be jealous?

MARK: It's getting late. I must go.

JUDY: You would be, wouldn't you? It doesn't make sense... After all, you're gay.

MARK: What's that got to do with it?

JUDY: What d'you think? *(MARK looks disappointed and gets up to go)* Come and sit down. *(JUDY pats the sofa for MARK to sit next to her)* But then, who knows, maybe your not as gay as you make out.

MARK: *(mirks)* Now that would be telling.

JUDY: Can I ask you a personal question?

MARK: *(smiles)* Nothing's stopped you so far. Ask me anything you like dear... Fire away!

JUDY: Have you ever been to bed with a woman?

MARK: What? Surely, sex isn't everything?

JUDY: *(looks at JUDY to see her reaction. JUDY seems confused)* No, I suppose it's not.

MARK: *(puts his arm around her)* Not if you are really fond of someone.

JUDY: You mean?

MARK: Yes. *(They stare at each other. As MARK turns away, JUDY goes to kiss him on the cheek, but he turns back, and she accidentally kisses him on the lips. MARK pulls away. JUDY is embarrassed and goes to speak, but instead MARK embraces her. MARK stops suddenly and stands up)* Please... I can't do this. *(looks down at his stomach)* I'm so sorry... Not like this.

JUDY: No, it's me who should apologise. Please, just forget it ever happened! I was being typically naive, stupid, little Judy.

MARK: It really isn't that important, is it?

JUDY: *(puts on a brave face)* No, of course not. Of course it isn't. Oh, dear! Now I feel really stupid. *(The doorbell rings and MARK freezes)*

MARK: Don't answer it!

JUDY: *(gets up to answer the door)* What?

MARK: *(becomes tense)* I said, don't answer it!

JUDY: Don't be stupid! Why not?

MARK: Because I've a good idea who it is...

JUDY: Really? And who the hell are you expecting at this time of night?

MARK: *(The doorbell goes again)* Do me a favour, and just don't answer it... *(begins switching the lights off, whispers)* Just pretend you're out.

JUDY: *(whispers back)* Why? And why are we whispering?

MARK: Ssh, just keep quiet and he'll go away.

JUDY: He? Who is he exactly?

MARK: Don't be an idiot... Matt of course!

JUDY: That's ridiculous! *(MARK goes to switch off the last light)* Leave that on, otherwise we'll be whispering in the dark! *(JUDY speaks normally)* Now, come on! Pull yourself together. It's only Roger on the scrounge for some milk.

MARK: It's not Roger...

JUDY: Well, if it's who you think it is, then answer the door.

MARK: I can't do that.

JUDY: In that case, I'll answer it. It's bound to be Roger.

MARK: *(As JUDY heads toward the door. MARK grabs her)* No, please don't!

JUDY: Be realistic! If it were your friend, how would he know you are here? *(MARK releases her)* You've just spooked yourself talking about him, that's all.

MARK: Maybe, but I'm not taking any chances.

JUDY: Then, at least put the lights back on. *(switches on the other lights and see's that MARK is very nervous)* My goodness, you're shaking? *(puts her arms on his shoulder)* Now, come on! I'm going to open the door and you'll see it's only Roger.

MARK: *(shrugs her off and goes over to the kitchen)* Before you do, just give me a couple of minutes to slip out through the kitchen.

JUDY: Don't be so foolish... There's no way out there.

MARK: Yes there is. Out the window and down the fire escape... Easy!

JUDY: Now, you really are being absurd.

MARK: I'm not... Please just trust me.

JUDY: Then, on your head be it... And if you survive, I'll see you in the morning. *(as MARK leaves JUDY calls after him)* Oh, and tomorrow, use the front door! *(MARK exits)*

MARK: *(V.O.)* Will do... See you in the morning.

JUDY: *(puts the other lights back on. The doorbell rings again. She goes to the fridge, takes out some milk and walks over to the front door)* Alright, I'm coming. *(opens the door)* Roger, you'll never know the problems you caused.

ROGER: *(As ROGER enters, JUDY hands him the milk)* Oh, thanks! Sorry, but I didn't mean to, I just picked it up by mistake.

JUDY: Picked what up?

ROGER: Mark's bag. *(holds up MARK'S bag)* I thought it was my baccy pouch. Sorry. *(goes over to the table and picks up his pouch and puts down his milk and MARK'S bag. As he does so, something drops out of the bag. ROGER doesn't notice and walks back to the front door)* I must say, it's difficult to fill a pipe with what some men keep in their bags these days.

JUDY: You don't care much for Mark, do you?

ROGER: It's not a question of like or dislike. I don't know him well enough to make a judgement. I usually get on with most chaps though.

JUDY: But you hardly speak to him.

ROGER: *(smiles)* Be fair, I barely get a chance, he's always too busy talking. But I admit, I do have an uncanny feeling that there is something not quite right about him.

JUDY: That's stating the obvious. He's just different, that's all.

ROGER: It's not that. I suppose, if the truth be known, I'm not sure I'd trust him. To be frank, I agree with Kate, I think he's hiding something...

JUDY: *(interrupts)* Roger, the same could be said of you. With your tweed jackets and pipe. You dress more like an old man rather than your own age group. Like you, Mark's just a little eccentric. *(smiles)*

ROGER: You don't really think I'm hiding something, do you?

JUDY: No, not really. But I do think you are jumping to conclusions. After all, you hardly know him.

ROGER: I suppose you're right. Maybe I'm judging a book by it's cover and all that.

JUDY: Yes, and that reminds me. A good book and an early night is exactly what I need. It's been quite an evening. *(steers ROGER back toward the door)* I'll see you soon.

ROGER: Sounds like a good idea. By the way, I'm sorry about the mix up. *(JUDY looks confused)* With Mark's bag?

JUDY: Oh, I see... Well, goodnight then.

ROGER: You too, sleep well. *(ROGER exits. JUDY closes the front door and walks back toward the sofa, then notices ROGER has left his milk and smiles. The doorbell rings. JUDY picks up the milk and goes to the door and opens it. She is taken aback by a figure standing in the hallway, unseen except for his shadow)*

MATTHEW: Hi, I'm Matthew. Is Mark here?

CURTAIN

END OF ACT I

ACT II

SCENE I

Judy's drawing room - evening. Continuation of the last scene.

MATTHEW: *(MATTHEW steps forward into the entrance. He is extremely good looking with dark hair. He is casually, but smartly dressed)* Sorry, have I come at a bad moment?

JUDY: *(completely taken aback)* My God... *(MATTHEW grins as JUDY becomes flustered)* Yes... Yes, I'm afraid you have...

MATTHEW: I'm sorry.

JUDY: Anyway, you've just missed him.

MATTHEW: Who?

JUDY: Mark of course!

MATTHEW: Oh, that's good.

JUDY: Good? *(looks back toward the kitchen)* What d'you mean, good?

MATTHEW: *(smiles)* Because it's you I came to see.

JUDY: Me?

MATTHEW: Yes, you.

JUDY: But why?

MATTHEW: Because, I have something to tell you...

JUDY: But you don't even know me.

MATTHEW: Can I come in?

JUDY: *(appears confused)* What?

MATTHEW: It is rather important.

JUDY: No...

MATTHEW: Just for a few minutes, that's all.

JUDY: *(looks around to see if MARK really has gone)* No, I'm sorry... I don't think so. Maybe when Mark is here.

MATTHEW: If I'd come to see him, I would have gone to his place.

JUDY: *(surprised)* You know where he lives?

MATTHEW: I've a pretty good idea.

JUDY: Then why come here? D'you want me to pass a message to him?

MATTHEW: No, no, I don't.

JUDY: Then why are you here?

MATTHEW: To talk to you... To tell you something.

JUDY: Me? I don't understand... This is all very unnerving.

MATTHEW: Why?

JUDY: Obviously, you just turning up, and at this time of night... I was just going to bed.

MATTHEW: I'm sorry, but I had to make sure you were alone.

JUDY: *(seems nervous)* Really? Well, I can easily get help if I need it.
MATTHEW: *(chuckles)* That won't be necessary. I assure you I'm perfectly harmless. And as I say, it is important.

JUDY: No, I'm sorry, come back in the daytime. When Mark's here.... *(goes to close the door)*

MATTHEW: But it's you I need to see... Please, just a couple of minutes, that's all.

JUDY: What could you possibly have to tell me that's so important? After all, I don't even know you.

MATTHEW: *(smiles at her)* But you will get to know me... I promise.

JUDY: I'm not sure I'd want to know you... So I'll say goodnight!

(Again JUDY goes to close the door but this time MATTHEW puts his foot in the way)

MATTHEW: Please... Just hear me out.

JUDY: *(looks down at his foot)* Since your foot seems to be firmly wedged in my front door, I suppose I've little choice in the matter. *(she opens the door wider)* You'd better come in then.

MATTHEW: *(enters, closes the door behind him. As he does, JUDY becomes nervous. MATTHEW walks over to the sofa and looks around)* I take it, Mark really isn't here?

JUDY: Of course he isn't. I wasn't lying.

MATTHEW: No, of course not. I'm sorry... Can I ask you something?

JUDY: And what is that exactly?

MATTHEW: Is it possible to have some water?

JUDY: Water?

MATTHEW: If it's no bother.

JUDY: To be honest, it is a bother. But I suppose, as you're here... *(goes to get MATTHEW some water)*

MATTHEW: Unless...

JUDY: Unless?

MATTHEW: You have something stronger?

JUDY: You're pushing your luck! *(looks at the drinks tray)* Ah, but it appears, you are out of luck, I'm afraid. *(begins to speak faster, as she checks through the bottles)* You see, my parents didn't really want me to move up here and with the cost of it all, there's not exactly a choice.

MATTHEW: I'm sorry, I didn't catch any of that?

JUDY: Forgive me, but do I tend to babble on a bit, especially when I'm nervous.

MATTHEW: Nervous?

JUDY: Well, not nervous exactly... Surprised.

MATTHEW: Yes, I suppose that's understandable.

JUDY: *(starts checking through the bottles again)* Ah, there's some cream sherry! But that's about all, I'm afraid.

MATTHEW: That's the second time you've used that word.

JUDY: Sherry?

MATTHEW: Afraid. You've said it twice. But you've no reason to be. I assure you, I'm perfectly harmless.

JUDY: *(ignores his remark)* Oh, it seems you are in luck! If you prefer, there's also some remnants of brandy.

MATTHEW: Brandy's perfect.

JUDY: *(As JUDY pours the brandy, her hand begins to tremble)* I'm glad you didn't want any of this sherry. My aunt says it can be awfully sickly.

MATTHEW: Sickly?

JUDY: It's very sweet.

MATTHEW: *(moves toward her and steadies her hand to stop it shaking)* I must admit, I rather like sweet things.

JUDY: But, you said you wanted brandy?

MATTHEW: I do.

JUDY: That's not sweet. *(MATTHEW looks into her eyes and grins. JUDY becomes embarrassed, as she realises he is making a pass, and so tugs her arm away)* Whatever you're up to, you can stop it right now! I'm not frightened of you.

MATTHEW: What? Why should you be?

JUDY: I'm warning you... I've only got to scream and my next door neighbour will come running.

MATTHEW: Your neighbour?

JUDY: Yes, he's just across the hall.

MATTHEW: Sorry, but you've lost me? I was only trying to steady your hand. You were shaking.

JUDY: Of course! It's only natural. A perfect stranger, no sooner comes through the door and makes a pass...

MATTHEW: That wasn't a pass. Either way, it's me who should be frightened.

JUDY: Of what exactly?

MATTHEW: Of your reaction... When I tell you why I came...

JUDY: Yes, and why did you come?

MATTHEW: It's about Mark...

JUDY: I thought so, well, if it's anything negative, you're wasting your time.

MATTHEW: But you have to listen to me.

JUDY: I don't have to listen to anything! If you've got something unpleasant to say, then you can tell him to his face... And if it is something I should know, he can always tell me in his own time.

MATTHEW: Don't you understand? He never will! *(bangs his glass down on the table. JUDY looks startled. MATTHEW calms himself)* Forgive me. I'm just tired, it's been a long day.

JUDY: *(seems a bit shocked)* I can certainly see why he's frightened of you.

MATTHEW: Frightened of me? *(chuckles)* The only thing he's frightened of is reality.

JUDY: Well, he knew it was you at the door... That was real enough...

That's why he fled.

MATTHEW: Oh, I see? So now, our Mark's developed extra sensory perception?

JUDY: Who knows? Maybe he has... Either way, he wasn't acting. He was genuinely frightened of you.

MATTHEW: *(scoffs)* Rubbish! Take it from me, anything that comes out of Mark's mouth, you can take with a pinch of salt... No, make that a large bucket!

JUDY: Is that so? Well, I believe what he told me about you threatening him.

MATTHEW: *(smirks and then looks at his watch)* Look, I'd better go.

JUDY: Go? *(seems surprised)* So the reason you came here, was just to bad mouth him?

MATTHEW: Actually, there was something else...

JUDY: Oh? And what's that?

MATTHEW: It's not important... *(stares at her)* Another time perhaps.

JUDY: *(scoffs)* Another time? That sounds like some form of ploy.

MATTHEW: Ploy?

JUDY: *(looks around)* I wouldn't be surprised, if you've dropped a handkerchief around here somewhere.

MATTHEW: A handkerchief?

JUDY: Or something equally as obvious... such as a glove.

MATTHEW: I don't understand?

JUDY: As an excuse for you to come back here.... At least it would have been more subtle, than pretending there was something else.

MATTHEW: Oh, I see. *(grins)* I think you'll find that's more of a woman's game.

JUDY: Is that so? Well then, as a man, you're in a perfect position to enlighten me... As to what your game is.

MATTHEW: Mine? Well, there isn't one. I'm serious, there really is something else that you should know.

JUDY: Really? Then tell me.

MATTHEW: *(finishes his drink and goes toward the door)* For now, it's best I leave and let you to get some sleep.

JUDY: Sleep?

MATTHEW: As you said, it is getting late... And you did say, you were just going to bed...

JUDY: Yes, but just how am I meant to get to sleep now?

MATTHEW: Easily, lie down and close your eyes... It works for me everytime.

JUDY: You can at least give me a clue, as to what this something else is?

MATTHEW: I promise you I will... When we get to know each other better.

JUDY: Huh! And to think Mark said you were shy.

MATTHEW: Did he indeed?

JUDY: And a lot more besides...

MATTHEW: Yes, I bet he did!

JUDY: For instance, how you threatened to kill him. *(looks worried)* Or should I take that with a bucket of salt, too?

MATTHEW: Oh, that... Yes, well that is true... But to be fair, we both said things we didn't mean... It was just said in the heat of the moment.

JUDY: Funny enough, that's exactly what I told him.

MATTHEW: *(seems relieved)* There we are then. And that's why I came, to straighten things out.

JUDY: Even so, what on earth has any of it got to do with me?

MATTHEW: *(opens the front door)* As I say, I'll explain when I get to know you better.

JUDY: What gives you the idea that I'd want you to get to kow me better?

MATTHEW: *(looks at her and grins)* You.

JUDY: Me?

MATTHEW: Yes... *(continues staring at JUDY)* So, I'll take it, I can drop by again sometime. Or would you prefer I call first?

JUDY: Neither! And I'm certainly not giving you my phone number.

MATTHEW: Fulham 0921... right?

JUDY: But how did...?

MATTHEW: You're in the directory.

JUDY: Mark said you liked reading, but he didn't mention it extended to telephone directories. Look, I think you'd better tell me what was this other reason you came here... Or just leave and don't come back.

MATTHEW: An ultimatum, eh? Now that's going to be a bit difficult, as I wanted tell you about Mark's little secret first... But you don't want to hear about that.

JUDY: Correct! So you can stop right there. So if there really is no other reason, you're here...You might as well leave right now.

MATTHEW: For what it's worth, I was only trying to help.

JUDY: Maybe, but as far as I'm concerned, if Mark is, as you say, hiding something, then, if he wants to, he can tell me himself.

MATTHEW: Trust me, he will never do that.

JUDY: Trust you? Who? The mysterious stranger arriving in the dead of night, just to spill the beans on his old friend.

MATTHEW: I suppose, looking at it that way, it might seem a little strange to someone who doesn't know the truth.

JUDY: You mean, depending on whose version of the truth, is in fact the truth!

MATTHEW: Exactly!

JUDY: Well for one, I'm not in the telephone dirctory, as I've just moved in!

MATTHEW: I know.

JUDY: You know? So how did you really get my number?

MATHEW: *(laughs as he points to a scrap of paper on a side table)* You've made a note of it on there.

JUDY: Yes, well unlike you, I haven't yet memorised it. Out of interest, what other little tricks you have up yours sleeve?

MATTHEW: Me? Tricks...? Now that would be telling... And certainly a good excuse to come back.

JUDY: *(smiles)* I'm not so sure about that.

MATTHEW: *(MATTHEW grins)* So I take it, I can come back?

JUDY: No way! But you're persistent, I'll give you that... *(MATTHEW stares at JUDY and smiles. JUDY becomes flustered again)* Well... maybe... We'll just have to see.

MATTHEW: See what?

JUDY: How things turn out between you and Mark.

MATTHEW: *(seems disappointed)* Yes, of course...

JUDY: Incidentally, when did you last see him?

MATTHEW: Ages ago, when we lived in Bristol.

JUDY: You don't live there anymore?

MATTHEW: No, I live in London.

JUDY: So you followed him up here?

MATTHEW: Not at all. I lost my job, so I came to London to find work.

JUDY: I'm sorry... What is it you did, or do for a living?

MATTHEW: You're very inquisitive...

JUDY: Not usually, but I'll sleep better, knowing I haven't let a complete lunatic into my flat.

MATTHEW: *(Laughs)* Lunatic? No, I'm not. Well, I'm certainly not mad, I can assure you.

JUDY: Good! Then you can tell me that other reason, you say you came here to tell me.

MATTHEW: As I said, all in good time. But for now, you can ask me anything else!

JUDY: Like what for instance?

MATTHEW: I don't know. Whatever you like. Whatever will put your mind at rest. *(JUDY looks at him suspiciously, then closes the* front door)

JUDY: *(they go and sit in the armchairs)* Yes, who knows? It just might.

MATTHEW: Well, then, go ahead! What d'you want to ask?

JUDY: What about answering my first question? What do you do for a living?

MATTHEW: Computer operator... Next question?

JUDY: Okay... And you're not working at present?

MATTHEW: No, I already told you.

JUDY: Yes, you did. Sorry...

MATTHEW: No need to be... Go on, fire away!

JUDY: Okay, let me think... I know. What, for you, is a typical day?

MATTHEW: No, that's boring!

JUDY: Really, why?

MATTHEW: Because I'm not working.

JUDY: Well, that might be more interesting...

MATTHEW: Being out of work?

JUDY: Yes.

MATTHEW: Are you sure it's not you that's crazy?

JUDY: No! How you fill your days, that might be interesting.

MATTHEW: Not really. I'm like most people, I suppose. Except, every morning, I go jogging just to ease the monotony. And, if en-route I pass a milk float, I purloin a bottle of full cream for my breakfast.

JUDY: Meaning you steal it?

MATTHEW: Of course not, I pay for it... If the milkman happens to catch me, that is.

JUDY: That's terrible... I'm sure most people don't steal their milk?

MATTHEW: That's because most people can't run as fast. Then when I get home, I strip completely naked...

JUDY: *(embarrassed)* That's too much information!

MATTHEW: *(looks at JUDY and grins)* And take a long, hot, soapy shower...

JUDY: You're right. This is boring. I'm not interested in what you have for breakfast, and even less so, in your bathing habits.

MATTHEW: You did ask.

JUDY: I asked, 'what, for you, is a typical day?'

MATTHEW: *(laughs)* And I gave you, what for me is a typical morning. So what now? Would you like to hear about my afternoons??

JUDY: No! I was just trying to find out more about you in general.

MATTHEW: Okay then, let me think...

JUDY: No rush, I'm surprisingly wide awake now.

MATTHEW: As I said, by profession I'm a computer operator... And before I lost my job, I was on about £48.00 a week, before tax. Then there is a deduction of £7.00 a week for my flat.

JUDY: Which is where exactly?

MATTHEW: Not far from here... Munster Road, number 26.

JUDY: I know where that is...

MATTHEW: *(smiles)* Flat 4. In case you're interested?

JUDY: *(ignores the question)* Is it nice?

MATTHEW: It's small, but very comfy. *(MATTHEW looks at JUDY and winks)* With a large double bed. You're very welcome to drop by and check it out anytime...

JUDY: *(blushes)* No thanks...

MATTHEW: I meant the flat. It's an open invitation. *(JUDY looks to the heavens)*

JUDY: For some reason, I'm suddenly more interested in your outgoings.

MATTHEW: Really? Well, after my rent, if you add on another £2.50 a week for my electric meter, with an insatiable appetite for 50 pence pieces, I'm left with very little spending money. So you see, the occasional free bottle of milk counts as a luxury in my dreary life. Especially now that I'm not working.

JUDY: That's still no excuse for stealing.

MATTHEW: It's not stealing, it's just a game.

JUDY: Maybe to you, but by other peoples standards, you're not exactly broke.

MATTHEW: But I am.

JUDY: How can you be?

MATTHEW: Because I've hardly any savings, as I like to go to football, especially to see Chelsea play... And that's not cheap.

JUDY: *(unimpressed)* Football?

MATTHEW: You're so lucky, their stadium is practically on your doorstep.

JUDY: To be honest, I find sport very boring.

MATTHEW: I'm in good company then, as most people find me boring.

JUDY: I didn't say that. So are you trying to get work?

MATTHEW: I have a promise of a new job.

JUDY: When does that start?

MATTHEW: Not sure; in a few weeks, but it's worth waiting for. It'll be double the pay and much better prospects.

JUDY: Now, that is interesting.

MATTHEW: Meaning I'm not?

JUDY: How would I know? Apart from what you've just told me, I know hardly anything about you...

MATTHEW: Oh, come on! I'm sure Mark's filled you in.

JUDY: Mark? Oh, yes, we've rather gotten off the subject of dear old Mark... So let me ask you something else then.

MATTHEW: Go for it.

JUDY: Why is he so frightened of you?

MATTHEW: It's not me. He's frightened of... As I said, Mark is just frightened of facing up to reality.

JUDY: But if he doesn't want to, why should he? Let's face it, we all see life as we want to see it. And that leads me to another question.

MATTHEW: Okay?

JUDY: After all this time? Why are you trying to come back into his life?

MATTHEW: Because I think it would be good for both of us to finally straighten things out.

JUDY: Yes, it just might be. After all, life's too short to bear grudges.

MATTHEW: What's more, I can help him, if he'll let me.

JUDY: How exactly?

MATTHEW: Be honest, don't you find the way he carries on ridiculous?

JUDY: No, I like the way he behaves... It's fun!

MATTHEW: *(disappointed)* Look, I'd better go. It's getting late.

JUDY: *(looks at her watch)* Gosh, yes it certainly is.

MATTHEW: I'll say goodnight then. *(gets up to leave)*

JUDY: Goodnight? No, hold on a moment! You still haven't told me if it's true...

MATTHEW: If what is?

JUDY: If there really was another reason you came here?

MATTHEW: Yes, there was...

JUDY: Then, why the mystery?

MATTHEW: Because, it's too embarrassing.

JUDY: Embarrassing? Now, I'm even more curious!

MATTHEW: Well, at least we have that in common.

JUDY: And what is that?

MATTHEW: Curiosity... I'm equally curious about you.

JUDY: Me?

MATTHEW: You were the other reason for me coming here tonight.

JUDY: But why?

MATTHEW: Because, when I heard Mark had got a job, I was surprised to say the least. So I became curious, as to who would employ him. Then, when I heard his employer was a beautiful young woman, I just had to come and see for myself.

JUDY: Then, you must have been so sorely disappointed.

MATTHEW: No, quite the contrary.

JUDY: *(embarrassed)* Oh, please, there's no point in trying to butter me up...! Ah, I get it now!

MATTHEW: Get what?

JUDY: I was right all along! It was just an excuse to come back.

MATTHEW: Well, to be honest, yes, it was.

JUDY: And to think you gave that big build up. Pretending it was something important.

MATTHEW: To me it is... I wasn't pretending... I was just too embarrassed to tell you.

JUDY: And so you should be. What a lot of nonsense and a waste of my time. I could have been in bed and fast asleep hours ago.

MATTHEW: Has it really been a waste of time?

JUDY: I don't know. I know I should be flattered. But quite frankly, I'm too tired to answer such a daft question... I'll have to sleep on it.
MATTHEW: Then, I'd best go and let you get your beauty sleep.

JUDY: Don't start that again... Oh, and before you go. Out of interest, how did you know, which was my flat number? My name's not on the bell.

MATTHEW: Your neighbour.

JUDY: Really? I'll kill him.

MATTHEW: Who?

JUDY: Roger.

MATTHEW: Who's Roger?

JUDY: My neighbour.

MATTHEW: No, it was a woman, on the ground floor. Very chatty she was.

JUDY: Oh, her? Yes, I know. She's a nice old thing, but dotty. She never closes that front door properly. *(looks at MATTHEW)* Anyone can just walk in.

MATTHEW: *(grins)* True! But she was right about one thing.

JUDY: Not to give out my flat number she wasn't.

MATTHEW: About you being beautiful.

JUDY: *(blushes)* Oh, come off it. Just stop trying to play on my vanity, that really is cheap!

MATTHEW: To be honest, she didn't actually say that...

JUDY: Thanks a lot!

MATTHEW: No, she said pretty... I say beautiful.

JUDY: *(blushing)* And what exactly am I meant to reply to that?

MATTHEW: How about, I can come back and see you again?

JUDY: *(MATTHEW moves closer to JUDY)* Oh, I don't know. Maybe, if Mark doesn't object. So you'd best speak to him about it first.

MATTHEW: But how can I, if he won't talk to me?

JUDY: That's not my problem. You'll just have to sort that out between yourselves.

MATTHEW: You know, I saw him the other day?

JUDY: Where?

MATTHEW: Outside the cinema.

JUDY: Did you speak to him?

MATTHEW: No...

JUDY: Why not?

MATTHEW: Because he just ran off.

JUDY: I'll have a word with him about that tomorrow. Anyway, this is still very strange. You just turning up here like this.

MATTHEW: I told you, it's about Mark, but you don't want to hear.

JUDY: Because it has nothing to do with me.

MATTHEW: I think you'll find, it has a lot to do with you. As I said, Mark likes his little secrets.

JUDY: *(They stand up and walk to the front door)* Don't we all. I like eating chocolate biscuits in bed... So what? Its hardly a crime.

MATTHEW: Really? *(grins)* No, but it does sound very enticing...

JUDY: It certainly wasn't meant to. So please, just say goodnight!

MATTHEW: *(Reluctantly)* Okay then... Goodnight.

JUDY: By the way, if... and I say this with a very small if, we do meet again, you'd best keep off that subject.

MATTHEW: Biscuits crumbs, in your bed?

JUDY: *(embarrassed)* You know exactly who I mean. As far as I'm concerned, any little secrets you might have between you, just leave them on the other side of that door...

MATTHEW: *(salutes)* Yes... Okay, noted!

JUDY: *(points to the front door)* Good. After all, it really isn't important.

MATTHEW: *(They look at each other)* It's funny you say that...

JUDY: Why?

MATTHEW: Because after meeting you, it doesn't seem to be.

JUDY: At least, something positive came out of your visit then.

MATTHEW: So does this mean, I can drop by again?

JUDY: I'll see how Mark feels about it. *(looks disappointed)*

JUDY: *(checks at her watch)* Gosh! Look at the time! Now I really have to get to bed. *(She notices MATTHEW is grinning)* Alone!

MATTHEW: Yes, of course. But be sure to tell him, I'll meet him whenever, or wherever he chooses.

JUDY: I will! I'll do that first thing tomorrow. *(she walks MAT-THEW to the door)*

MATTHEW: You promise?

JUDY: Yes, of course.

MATTHEW: I'll wish you goodnight then.

JUDY: *(opens the front door. They stare at each other andsmile)* Goodnight. *(slowly closes the door)*

LIGHTS FADE

END OF SCENE I

ACT II SCENE II

LIGHTS UP. Next morning. MARK lets himself in with his key and puts on the kettle. While he's waiting for it to boil, he pours some orange juice and takes it over to JUDY, who is still sleeping. MARK gently touches her with the cold glass to wake her.

JUDY: Oh, no, it's not morning already?

MARK: Take another couple of minutes to open those big beautiful eyes and it'll be afternoon.

JUDY: *(Sits up)* What? Afternoon?

MARK: Midday, to be precise!

JUDY: *(gets out of bed and goes to put on her slippers but only finds one)* Where's my other slipper?

MARK: How would I know? I said midday, not midnight... So you couldn't have lost it leaving the ball.

JUDY: Is that supposed to be a joke?

MARK: Oh, dear, we are in a bad mood... Have a look, it's probably under the bed. *(JUDY rummages under the bed)* D'you know the real truth about Cinderella?

JUDY: No jokes, not this morning... *(retrieves her slipper from under the bed, then glances at the bedside clock)* Even if it is the afternoon.

MARK: Oh, come on, you'll like this.

JUDY: *(not listening)* Oh, blast. I've missed lunch with Kate. Why didn't you wake me sooner?

MARK: Because I've only just sailed through that door, dear. *(JUDY puts on her dressing gown and heads to the kitchen area, where MARK is making the tea)* Look, I'm sorry, but it's the first time I've been late in ages. Now, come on. Crack a little smile. It just might cure that poker face.

JUDY: *(As JUDY scowls, MARK gently pulls her in front of a mirror. She then begins to smile)* I'm sorry, I didn't mean to snap like that. But last night was quite a night.

MARK: *(goes over to the bed area and finds her other slipper and waves it)* I may not be your idea of Prince Charming, but you could at least listen to my little joke.

JUDY: Not now...

MARK: What do you mean, not now?

JUDY: I said, not now... Maybe later.

MARK: *(waves the slipper)* Then you don't get your slipper back. *(JUDY looks to the heavens)* Before Cinderella set off to the ball, her fairy godmother gave her a word of warning. *(JUDY reluctantly listens, as MARK hands her the slipper. He then finishes making the tea)* 'Beware,' she said, 'make sure that you are back by midnight, otherwise your pussy will turn into a pumpkin'.

JUDY: Mark!

MARK: *(hands JUDY her tea)* Ssh, be quiet and listen. At the ball, Cinderella dances all night, with none other than Prince Charming himself. But, unbeknownst to her, the prince was stunned more by her dress than her beauty. He offered her all kinds of precious jewels, if only she would let him try it on.

JUDY: Oh, Mark honestly...

MARK: Ssh..! Cinderella was tempted by the offer, and, after all, she thought, what harm could come of humouring yet another would - be faggot? As she already had one at home... And he was just her cleaner.

JUDY: *(becomes annoyed)* What? Now, Mark, just stop!

MARK: Well, she did. Anyway, back to the plot. Just as Cinderella was about to let him get into her dress, she noticed the time. It was five minutes to midnight. Remembering her fairy godmother's warning, 'be home by midnight!'she upped her skirt and fled. But in her panic, Cinderella tripped and lost her slipper. Luckily for her, a handsome young courtier saw her drop it and quickly picked it up.

JUDY: Oh, come on! We all know the story... And they lived happily ever after!

MARK: Sssh! As the courtier handed Cinderella the slipper, he asked her for one quick dance. She explained why she had no time. Then, as she truned to leave, Cinderella asked him his name.

JUDY: And he answered, Prince Charming!

MARK: *(glowers at JUDY)* No! He answered, 'I'm Peter, Peter, the Pumpkin Eater!' To which Cinderella replied, 'In that case, forget the time... We can dance all night! *(Mark laughs as JUDY feigns a smile)*

JUDY: Okay, you've told your little joke. Now pull yourself together. I have to tell you about last night. *(JUDY walks over to the sofa)* Now, come and sit down.

MARK: Well, let me get my tea and then we can get cosy. *(goes to the kitchen gets his tea)*

JUDY: The tea can wait.

MARK: If you're gonna sack me, I might as well fortify myself first.

JUDY: Sack you? Who said anything about sacking you?

MARK: Well, that's a relief.

JUDY: For a change, will you just listen?

MARK: Honey, I'm all ears. I'm hanging on every word. *(brings his tea over and puts it on the coffee table)*

JUDY: Will you be serious?

MARK: *(grins)* I always am.

JUDY: Now just stop it... Get real for once.

MARK: Reality is exactly what I plan to see, but not today... Oh, come on... Whatever's wrong, it can't be that bad.

JUDY: Matthew was here last night.

MARK: *(frowns)* It is that bad... I told you, it was him.

JUDY: No, that was Roger. He'd come for some milk and to return your bag. Evidently, he mistook it for his baccy pouch. *(JUDY hands MARK his bag; MARK grabs it and starts sorting through the contents)* I'm sure he didn't steal anything. Anyway, that's not important. After he left, there was another ring at the door. When I opened it, standing in the doorway was Matthew. *(MARK appears disinterested and continues on rummaging)* By the way, you never told me he was that handsome.

MARK: I did... Now a nice chocolate biccy is what you need. *(hands JUDY a biscuit, but she brushes it aside and puts down her mug)*

JUDY: You were right... He's everything a girl could wish for... Tall, dark...

MARK: And handsome. Everything I'm not, I suppose?

JUDY: I didn't mean that. *(MARK continues rummaging through his bag)* What is it with you? Last night you flew out of here terrified, because you thought he was outside. And now I tell you that he was, you don't appear to be remotely interested.

MARK: Because I have a pretty good idea why he was here...

JUDY: Meaning?

MARK: You of course...

JUDY: Me?

MARK: And what's more, you fell for it... Or should I say him?

JUDY: What are you on about? Why on earth would you even say that?

MARK: What was it you just said? He's everything a girl could wish for.

JUDY: That was just a figure of speech... You know what I mean.

MARK: Sadly, I think I do.

JUDY: Oh, really?

MARK: Why d'you think I told you not to open that door?

JUDY: Because you were scared... You said, he'd threatened to kill you... Or did that slip your mind?

MARK: That too, of course. I just didn't want to take the chance in case he was serious.

JUDY: Then you can relax, because he wasn't. All he was doing was trying to patch things up between you...

MARK: Oh, really?

JUDY: Yes, really. He just wants to make friends, that's all.

MARK: Well, that's about as likely as you and I going on a date together!

JUDY: *(chuckles)* I can think of worse things...

MARK: *(looks surprised)* Now, that would be weird!

JUDY: *(shrugs)* I suppose it would...

MARK: Be truthful! Looks aside, didn't you find him just the teeny weeniest bit dull?

JUDY: Not at all. In fact, I thought he was rather endearing. *(picks up a key from the floor)* What's this?

MARK: *(looks relieved)* Oh, there it is. That's mine, give it to me. *(snatches it from her hand)* It must have dropped out of my bag.

JUDY: What does it open that's so important?

MARK: Oh, just my very own Pandora's box.

JUDY: He'll be back, you know?

MARK: Of course he will.

JUDY: And that's another thing, he was nothing like you'd described him.

MARK: How come? You just told me how good looking you thought he was.

JUDY: I mean, he certainly wasn't shy... You said he was. In fact he was quite the opposite.

MARK: Then, if you want my advice, if he does return, don't let him in. I'm telling you... He's trouble.

JUDY: Nonsense! He was no trouble last night...

MARK: How long was he here for?

JUDY: At least a couple of hours. And in all that time, he was the perfect gentleman. I really think you should meet him. Give him a second chance so to speak.

MARK: Are you crazy? Best you don't answer that!

JUDY: He's agreed to meet up, wherever suits you. I can't see what the problem is. This could be the perfect opportunity to bury the hatchet.

MARK: Yes, and I know exactly where. You can't be serious?

JUDY: Deadly serious.

MARK: An unfortunate choice of words.

JUDY: I think it would be good for you both.

MARK: It sounds to me, you really have fallen for him.

JUDY: Well, maybe just a bit... But not in that way.

MARK: Oh, and in what way is that then?

JUDY: I'll admit, he is very sexy... And to be perfectly honest, I wouldn't mind seeing him again.

MARK: And do I get a vote on this?

JUDY: Yes, of course you do.

MARK: Then it's a no!

JUDY: That settles it then. I won't. *(looks very disappointed)* It's a shame though, as he's really quite sweet... With those piercing blue eyes and that thick dark hair... He really is a hunk.

MARK: You're beginning to repeat yourself.

JUDY: Not to mention, he's the first good-looking man that I've met in London.

MARK: *(MARK sees that JUDY is disappointed)* Okay, I'm getting the message. *(cups his hands over his ears)* The vibes are beginning to come through loud and clear. Oh, my god! They're getting even stronger! *(takes his hands away from his ears and looks serious)* Do you really want to see him again?

JUDY: Stop teasing, I just told you I'd like to. But not if you disapprove. So that's the end of the matter.

MARK: Then it seems, I'll have to give this some serious thought.. You'll have to give me time to think about it.

JUDY: Yes, of course... Take all the time you need. And afterwards, if it's still a no... then we won't discuss it ever again.

MARK: *(slowly stands up and looks at JUDY. He then adopts different ballet positions. He places one foot infront of the other with his heels touching and his toes turned out. Then bends his knees, extends one arm to his side and one toward JUDY. He then places one foot behind him, before bringing it up to the side of his other knee. Standing on one foot, he stares at JUDY as if in deep thought)*

JUDY: *(bewildered)* What on earth are you doing?

MARK: Thinking! *(MARK suddenly raises his arms above his head lowers his leg and does a pirouette)* There we are!

JUDY: What d'you mean? 'there we are'

MARK: I've thought about it... On second thoughts, go for it! If he does turn up again... See him!

JUDY: That was quick! But you just said?

MARK: Just call me a fickle.

JUDY: Seriously, d'you think I should? *(smiles)*

MARK: Yes, but on one condition!

JUDY: Which is?

MARK: I don't have to see him again.

JUDY: Okay, but I wish you would.

MARK: Either way, go for it! See if I care.

JUDY: But you do... Don't you?

MARK: Of course I do. But I'm not bothered, because I know it won't last... Just like the others, you'll get bored with him soon enough.

JUDY: So, you really wouldn't mind, if I met him again?

MARK: Oh, please! D'you want it written in ink, or d'you prefer blood?

JUDY: Okay, if he does show up again, then I will.

MARK: He ceratinly will. You can bank on it.

JUDY: Good.

MARK: Having given it so much thought, I now realise this might just work out rather nicely.

JUDY: I hope so...

MARK: Because you know what they say about keeping your friends close and your enemies...

JUDY: Closer. But he's not your enemy.

MARK: Maybe, but at least you can keep me updated as to what he's really up to.

JUDY: I'd rather you just met him. Then you won't need a go-between.

MARK: No way. So what else did he have to say for himself?

JUDY: Oh, now all of a sudden, you're interested? As it happens, he just went on about you having a secret.

MARK: *(becomes anxious)* Did he indeed?

JUDY: Do you have a secret?

MARK: Of course not! Did he say what this so-called secret was?

JUDY: No. But thinking about it, it was all a bit odd...

MARK: Odd? In what way?

JUDY: At first, he said it was important. But then he changed his mind.

MARK: Did he say why?

JUDY: He claimed that after meeting me, it didn't seem to be so important.

MARK: That is odd... And that's all he said?

JUDY: Yes, he didn't pursue it after that.

MARK: It doesn't make any sense.

JUDY: You're right! Mind you, I did tell him, if it was anything unpleasant about you, I didn't want to hear.

MARK: You've known me long enough to know I have no secrets...

JUDY: Even if you do, it's none of my business.

MARK: If you ask me, I think it was just an excuse to come here... He obviously fancies you.

JUDY: *(blushes)* Absolute rubbish!

MARK: Well, you did say, he lost interest in me fast enough. Come off it... You know he does.

JUDY: *(JUDY still blushing)* Of course he doesn't?

MARK: Either way, just be careful.

JUDY: Of what exactly?

MARK: That'll be for to you to find out.

JUDY: Well, he certainly must have changed since you last saw him.

MARK: In what way?

JUDY: Why not meet him and see for yourself?

MARK: No way. What else did he have to say for himself.

JUDY: Only, that he's in computers. Also, he doesn't appear to have many friends in London.

MARK: *(laughs)* But he's never had any friends!

JUDY: At least, I can sympathise with him there.

MARK: Come on, I'm sure old Roger considers himself your friend.

JUDY: Old Roger, that's just it. He's not old, but he behaves as if he is. The only reason he invites me out, is to fill one of his complimentary seats.

MARK: At least he invites you...

JUDY: Yes, then always drops me back home, without so much as a drink, let alone a kiss.

MARK: Well you should tell him. Scream at him, after the concert, 'Judy would now like a nice dinner and a big stiff...!

JUDY: Stop it! There are times, Mark, you go too far!

MARK: Drink! I was only trying to help.

JUDY: Anyway, I'd never dare.

MARK: Why not?

JUDY: He would probably collapse at the thought of little Judy not being the naive, silly girl, everybody seems to think I am.

MARK: Why bother going out with him then?

JUDY: For the company. When you're not around, it's either Roger, or sitting here on my tod.

MARK: *(sarcastically)* Cheer up, the way things are going, you'll soon have the lovely Matthew for company. *(MARK looks into the chute in the kitchen)* I'd still love to know how he knew I'd be here?

JUDY: He said he saw you outside the cinema.

MARK: *(thinks for a moment)* So it was him? I thought it was...

JUDY: When was this?

MARK: Yesterday.

JUDY: Why didn't you say something?

MARK: Because I wasn't sure. It all happened so quickly. It was as I was passing that cinema on the Fulham Road. You know the one, where they're showing, *The Exorcist*.

JUDY: I wish you had told me you were going to the pictures. I could have come with you, I love a good horror film.

MARK: I said, I was passing. That's when I thought I saw him coming out.

JUDY: He said you ran away. Is that true?

MARK: Of course I did. I thought I'd lost him, obviously I didn't.

JUDY: You should have spoken to him.

MARK: *(ignores JUDY'S comment and starts emptying the rubbish down the chute)* That must be how he knew I worked here... He followed me. *(again he looks down into the chute, then turns to JUDY)* It's like the Blackwall Tunnel down there.

JUDY: Yes, be careful; it's a long drop.

MARK: What's at the bottom?

JUDY: I think there's an enormous dustbin. It holds all the rubbish for the block.

MARK: *(pushes a large black plastic bag down the chute)* You could fit a body in here. *(keeps peering down the shoot)* How often does it get emptied?

JUDY: The bin? Once a week. A large lorry picks it all up and takes it away. Why are we talking about rubbish?

MARK: I wasn't, you were. *(walks back into the living room)* You said, Matthew stayed for how long?

JUDY: I suppose it must have been well over two hours in the end. Then he finished his brandy and left.

MARK: Just like that?

JUDY: No, in fact, I told him to go.

MARK: Why?

JUDY: Because it was getting very late.

MARK: So what did you do in all that time?

JUDY: We just chatted... Then, when I saw how late it was, that's when I asked him to leave. I really needed to get some sleep.

MARK: I see... Well, promise me one thing.

JUDY: What's that?

MARK: It won't affect our friendship.

JUDY: What won't?

MARK: You seeing him.

JUDY: Of course it wouldn't. Why would it?

MARK: It's just, I'd hate anything to change between us, that's all.

JUDY: Don't be so silly, I wouldn't let it.

MARK: But, if he does start coming around, things just might. Especially, if you fall for him.

JUDY: *(laughs)* Oh, come off it! I think you're getting ahead of yourself. Give me a break. I've only just met him...

MARK: As you said, stranger things have happened. I recently read in that magazine. *(points to a magazine on the coffee table)* Some gullible rich old woman fell for a Spanish waiter. She married him, and after their first date, he emptied her bank account... She never saw him again.

JUDY: Fat chance of that! I'm certainly not old... And I'm definitely not rich!

MARK: Yes, but you have to admit, you are gullible.

JUDY: You're beginning to sound like Kate. Don't believe everything you read in *Woman's Weekly.* Besides, I'm hardly going to fall head over heels in love... It's just a date, that's all.

MARK: Date? That's it... There we are... You've just said it.

JUDY: Said what?

MARK: Date... Not meet.

JUDY: *(flustered)* Date? Meet? What's the difference? You know what I mean.

MARK: Sadly, I think I do.

JUDY: Mark, I think it's time it got through that beautiful blond hair of yours, even our friendship has its limitations.

MARK: Because I'm gay, you mean?

JUDY: *(shapes her fingers as a gun and puts them to her temple)* Da! At last, the penny drops.

MARK: I'm not dumb. I get it. *(MARK stares at JUDY)*

JUDY: Good. Then understand this: What I don't need is another companion in my life... I have you for that.

MARK: Thanks...

JUDY: After all, who else could be so much fun? *(smiles)* But, I need more than just companionship.

MARK: Meaning a lover, I suppose?

JUDY: Not necessarily a lover as such... But to be perfectly frank, I do need sex... After all, I'm twenty four years old! I'd better find someone before it's too late.

MARK: What? Are you saying you haven't yet hit the sack with anyone?

JUDY: Sack?

MARK: Been between the sheets with a man?

JUDY: That's a crude way of putting it... And in any case, it's none of your business.

MARK: So, I can take it you haven't!

JUDY: You can take it how you like. But, as it happens, I did hit the sack, as you call it. When I was nineteen... I'm not an old maid!

MARK: You little minx. Come on then, tell all. What was he like? Was he blond? Muscular... tanned?

JUDY: No, he was as white as lard, skinny, and extremely spotty, with bright ginger hair.

MARK: Yuck! Where did you drag him up?

JUDY: He was a cadet from the local barracks... We'd known each other since nursery school.

MARK: A pale spotty youth, he sounds awful.

JUDY: Funny enough, I was very fond of him.

MARK: Really?

JUDY: But, then he went and spoiled it all... By falling in love...

MARK: Aah, sweet!

JUDY: With his Army career! *(chuckles)* It's not funny!

MARK: Sorry, of course not. So I guess you ended it?

JUDY: I didn't get the chance to. After a couple of weeks, he joined his regiment and marched off to Northern Ireland. I never saw him again.

MARK: Don't tell me and you've been celibate ever since?

JUDY: You do have a habit of asking the most embarrassing questions.

MARK: Come on, tell me...

JUDY: Let me put it this way. In Aldershot, there wasn't exactly a queue of handsome, eligible bachelors to choose from.

MARK: What about all those handsome soldiers?

JUDY: Yes, all hidden behind their uniforms... I can tell you, the ones I met weren't so handsome once they were out of them.

MARK; You naughty girl! So how many others did you manage to get out of their uniforms?

JUDY: You are incorrigible! None! I meant, when they were in their civvies. At least you could see what you're getting.

MARK: Pull the other one!

JUDY: It's true! Uniforms can be deceptive...

MARK: Aah, now the penny drops! So that's what this is all about...

JUDY: What d'you mean?

MARK: Don't be coy! Matthew, of course!

JUDY: That's absurd! What on earth's it got to do with him?

MARK: Well, he doesn't have a uniform. So, you know what you're getting... Or at least, you think you do.

JUDY: It was just an observation, that's all.

MARK: You just be careful. Knowing him, I wouldn't be surprised if he has some other form of uniform to hide behind.

JUDY: Well, if he has... I'm sure, I'll soon find out for myself.

MARK: And just you remember, don't come crying back to me when you do. Mark my words, and I mean, *(points to himself)* 'remember, mark Mark's words...!' Be careful.

JUDY: Of what exactly?

MARK: I think for now, it's probably best for me to know... And for you to find out for yourself.

CURTAIN

END OF SCENE II. ACT I.

ACT II SCENE I

LIGHTS UP. Day-time a couple of months later. JUDY is sitting on the sofa arranging flowers. MARK is making the bed and whistling 'Whistle While You Work' from Snow White)

JUDY: Mark, must you?

MARK: Must I what?

JUDY: Whistle.

MARK: Why? You never objected before.

JUDY: I never objected when you spoke either. *(MARK continues whistling)* Now you're just being stupid.

MARK: *(finishes making the bed)* Am I?

JUDY: You know you are. You're just doing it to annoy me.

MARK: You flatter yourself. I just happen to like the tune. *(begins to whistle again)*

JUDY: Just stop it!

MARK: Why? It's you who's being stupid, not me.

JUDY: Maybe, but at least I'm not whistling to pretend everything is alright.

MARK: Then perhaps it's you who should be whistling.

JUDY: Why don't you just come out with it? It's because of these, isn't it? *(finishes arranging the flowers)*

MARK: In a way, yes. Because since you've been seeing him, you've changed. It's as if you're in some kind of dream world.

JUDY: And while we're on the subject, since I've been seeing him, you've hardly spoken a word. Whenever you arrive, you just whistle your way around the flat, then leave as early as you can.

MARK: Of course I do, in case I bump into him... That's what we agreed, remember? I told you, I don't want to see him!

JUDY: I wish you'd stop all this nonsense and just meet up. It seems stupid... Especially, as it was you, who agreed that I should see him. *(MARK doesn't look pleased)* Come on, own up - there's something else bothering you.

ROGER: *(Doorbell goes and MARK opens the door)* Hello, Mark. As happy and gay as ever, are we? *(MARK frowns)* Sorry, have I come at a bad time?

JUDY: Not a bad time... *(JUDY nods toward MARK)* A bad mood.

MARK It's alright, I'm taking it with me. I'm off.

JUDY: You don't have to go.

ROGER: Please, don't leave on my account.

JUDY: He's not. Are you Mark?

MARK: That's right.

JUDY: He's leaving on someone else's.

MARK: No, I'm not. *(starts to put on his coat)*

JUDY: Of course you are. You haven't stayed over since I've been seeing him.

ROGER: *(appears embarrassed)* Look, I'd best go.

JUDY: No, sit down. *(ROGER lights up his pipe and sits on the sofa. JUDY looks over at MARK)* You too, come and sit down. *(MARK puts down his coat, and they sit either side of ROGER and talk across him)* Now, for what it's worth, he may be drop dead gorgeous... And I admit, he's wonderful in bed...

MARK: Stop right there! I don't want to hear!

JUDY: What I mean to say is, he's nothing like you.

MARK: Well, that's stating the obvious.

JUDY: D'you remember before his last visit? You spent hours doing my hair and making your mind up, as to which dress I should wear?

MARK: Of course, it took forever giving you a blow-dry and getting your frizzes out.

JUDY: Very funny.

MARK: I must admit though, it was worth it... And you did look stunning in that blue dress.

JUDY: Would you believe it? When he eventually deigned to arrive, he never noticed a thing.

MARK: You mean, after all my effort? Not even a compliment on that lovely dinner I cooked?

JUDY: Nope, nothing! He just gobbled down your chicken chasseur and that apple crumble, as if it was going to be his last meal...

MARK: I wish it had of been... It was that good, eh?

JUDY: No, it was so he wouldn't miss some cowboy film on the television.

MARK: What a cheek! That chasseur took me ages to prepare... Not to mention my crumble. I loathe him even more now. I knew I should have added some strychnin.

JUDY: Thanks, I ate some of it, too, remember?

MARK: Only joking.

JUDY: I hope so!

MARK: Well, at least it didn't go to waste.

JUDY: Ah, but then after 10.30... Now that's another story!

MARK: After 10.30?

JUDY: That's when the televion stations close down... It's bedtime!

MARK: Yes well, you can thank the good old miners strike for that!

JUDY: I do.

MARK: I can't believe television is more important to him than you are! What a moron that guy is.

JUDY: At least, he's good in bed, I'll give him that...

MARK: Oh, please, I really don't want to hear!

JUDY: I'm serious. That's when he comes into his own.

MARK: *(becomes embarrassed)* Well, you've certainly leapt out of your shell.

JUDY: *(winks at MARK)* I've had a great teacher remember? But, if I'm honest...

MARK: No don't be... I think you've been honest enough already.

ROGER: Perhaps a little too honest!

MARK: *(frowns at ROGER)* Who asked you?

JUDY: You were right on one thing.

MARK: Oh? At last, an accolade! And what is that exactly?

JUDY: He's not exactly a laugh a minute.

MARK: Surprise, surprise! I did warn you.

JUDY: All he talks about is computers.

MARK: I told you he was a bore...

JUDY: He says they are the future. They'll be like televisions... We'll all have one in our homes.

MARK: He always did talk rubbish! Have you seen the size of them? You wouldn't be able to get a computer up those stairs, let alone fit one in here.

JUDY: Other than that, all he talks about is sport... Or you, of course.

MARK: Me? Oh, so he's not a complete bore.

JUDY: If only he were more like you, then he'd be perfect!

MARK: Well, I can't argue with that.

JUDY: *(smiles)* It's a pity you're not straight.

ROGER: *(appears to be even more embarrassed and stands up)* This obviously is a bad moment.

JUDY: For what?

ROGER: To see if you're free tonight. I'll call you later.

JUDY: Well, I'm meant to be seeing Matthew, *(looks at MARK)* but I'm not sure I should.

MARK: Oh, please, don't put him off on my account.

ROGER: Or mine...

MARK: *(annoyed)* Come on Roger, we'd better go then. It'll take her hours to get ready, if he's coming.

JUDY: You mean, you're not going to help?

MARK: Not this time.

ROGER: Oh, by the way, Judy. Be very careful who you open the door to.

MARK: Your advice is a bit late, dear.

ROGER: I'm serious. The lock on the front door is loose, it doesn't shut properly. It's as if someone has tried to break in.

JUDY: Oh, dear...

ROGER: But don't worry, I'll fix it later.

JUDY: You are an angel, thank you. *(heads off toward the kitchen with the flowers)*

MARK: That's funny you mentioned that door, because yesterday, I saw two gay muggers attack an old lady right outside these very flats.

ROGER: That's terrible... But how did you know they were gay?

MARK: It was obvious, one was holding her down...

ROGER: Don't tell me... While the other one was blow-drying her hair!

MARK: *(surprised)* You are a dark horse! I wouldn't have thought you'd have known that joke ?

ROGER: Oh, come on, Mark, that joke, really is a very old chestnut!

MARK: Even so, I would never have given you credit for knowing it.

ROGER: *(turns and looks at MARK)* I'm sure there are a few things, you haven't yet, given me credit for knowing.

MARK: *(looks at ROGER suspiciously)* You're full of surprises, I'll give you that! *(laughs)* From now on, I had better my eye on you. *(ROGER and MARK leave and close the door)*

BLACKOUT END OF SCENE III

ACT II SCENE IV

(JUDY'S flat nighttime. JUDY is dressed to kill. Chopin is playing in the background.. As she pours a drink, she appears to be anxious.. Then, as she goes to sit in one of the armchairs, the phone rings)

JUDY: Oh, it's you, Roger. No, there's nobody here yet. Yes, okay. I'll see you on Friday. And tea afterwards? *(Sarcastically)* What a treat! Thanks, bye. *(The phone rings again. JUDY picks it up immediately)* Hello! No, Mark, he hasn't... I'm sure that's the reason you rang... To gloat! Then why else? No? Hold on. *(goes over to the fridge and brings out a bottle of wine. Then she picks up the phone)* My favourite Chardonnay, thank you. What d'you mean, it'll help? *(giggles)* Oh, I see. Anyway, I'm not waiting much longer, the dinner is already ruined. What d'you mean 'it couldn't be'? I'll have you know, I'm a very good cook! Yes, well, okay... See you in the morning... Bye. *(looks at her watch, then puts the wine back in the fridge. She then dims the lights in the living room and goes over to the bed area to change. She takes off her clothes and slips into a scanty dressing gown. She then moves down stage and sits in an armchair and idly thumbs through some magazines).* House Beautiful? Huh! My Mark could put this to shame! *(throws the magazine to the floor)* Rubbish! *(sifts through the other magazines on the table)* Men's Physique magazine? Oh, Mark... *(She thumbs through it)* They're all naked...! Mmm, what amazing physiques! *(puts down the magazine and gets into the bed. As the music becomes more sensual, she begins to slowly stroke her breasts over her nightie. The front door opens and MATTHEW walks into the*

138

room. He watches for a while in silence. Then whispers)

MATTHEW: Judy? *(gets no reaction, until he stumbles over a side table)* Ouch! *(JUDY quickly switches on the light. And as she gets off the bed, she turns off the music)*

JUDY: Damn you, Matthew! What the hell do you think you're doing creeping around?

MATTHEW: *(he is clutching a bottle of champagne and appears to be a little drunk)* But I wasn't...

JUDY: And how did you get in?

MATTHEW: With Mark's key of course. How do you think?

JUDY: He gave it to you?

MATTHEW: No, but you'd have been better entrusting me with it. When he leaves, he just tucks it on the ledge above your flat door. Anyone could use it.

JUDY: That's beside the point. *(looks at her watch)* You were meant to be here hours ago. So don't expect to eat... *(JUDY walks over to him)* And your breath reeks of alcohol... You're drunk!

MATTHEW: *(goes over to JUDY)* I'm sorry... I can explain.

JUDY: *(fans her face with her hand)* Don't bother.

MATTHEW: *(hugs the bottle of champagne and giggles)* I'm a naughty boy, I know. But it wasn't my fault.

JUDY: But you can't just walk in here, whenever it suits you... Especially in your state.

MATTHEW: But I come bearing good news!

JUDY: Good for you, but I'm not interested... So please leave.

MATTHEW: Leave? That's just it... I won't have to anymore.

JUDY: I just don't understand you, I really don't.

MATTHEW: Don't be silly. Come on, get some glasses and we can celebrate.

JUDY: Celebrate? Celebrate what exactly?

MATTHEW: That I'm no longer out of work. *(looks over at the dining table)* And you won't have to feed me anymore!

JUDY: *(sarcastically)* Oh, dear, so no more romantic evenings staring at the television?

MATTHEW: Oh, come on! I'm not that bad... Am I?

JUDY: Yes you are... Out of the sack that is...

MATTHEW: *(appears to be taken aback by her remark)* Sorry?

JUDY: Anyway, what is this new job?

MATTHEW: Oh, erm, the one I told you about. You know, developing software. And what's more, they are paying me a fortune... I mean, real money! I told you computers are the future.

JUDY: *(doesn't seem impressed)* It may be your future, but not mine.

140

MATTHEW: Come on, don't say that.

JUDY: But that's just it. Computers and sport, that's all you're really interested in.

MATTHEW: That's not true and you know it.

JUDY: Not forgetting your other favourite subject... And we both know who he is.

MATTHEW: Who?

JUDY: Mark, of course! You're like a double act!

MATTHEW:*(Scoffs)* That's rich coming from you! From the moment I arrive, all I hear is, 'Mark this, Mark that...' Oh, and of course, how wonderful Mark is.

JUDY: That's not fair. It's you who's always asking questions about him. I just answer them... And if that isn't bad enough, he does the same! What is it with you two?

MATTHEW: Does he indeed?

JUDY: You see? We're back to him again. But then to be fair, what else do we have to talk about?

MATTHEW: You could try my career for a start. Oh, sorry, I forgot. You're not interested in computers...

JUDY: No, I'm not... And you're not interested in the theatre.

MATTHEW: Touche! You're right. I'm not interested in the theatre... Or drama schools come to that. So maybe we both need to make more of an effort.

JUDY: I think it's too late for that.

MATTHEW: *(winks at JUDY and gestures toward the bedroom area)* Come on, you have to admit, it's not all bad...

JUDY: Yes, it really is! Well, most of the time... As I say, outside of the bedroom!

MATTHEW: Rubbish! What's suddenly brought all this on?

JUDY: I've had enough, I suppose.

MATTHEW: Of me?

JUDY: Of us, me being piggy in the middle between you two. You were supposed to have sorted things out weeks ago.

MATTHEW: But it was you who told me not to bother... To give him time to come around. Otherwise, believe me, I would have tried!

JUDY: Even so, if you were really going to, you'd have done it anyway.

MATTHEW: Okay, no problem... then I will tomorrow. *(attempts to kiss JUDY. But she rejects him)* What's wrong?

JUDY: I'm sorry, I'm not in the mood.

MATTHEW: Really? From what I just witnessed, *(gestures toward the bedroom)* you looked very much in the mood. Or was that exhibtion a sign that you weren't in the mood? Sorry, but I'm getting mixed signals here. *(attempts to kiss her again, JUDY pulls away)*

142

JUDY: Stop it!

MATTHEW: I don't understand?

JUDY: I would have thought it was obvious... I'm bored.

MATTHEW: You're beginning to sound just like the others.

JUDY: What others?

MATHEW: Other girls. They also said I was boring.

JUDY: I didn't say that, but to be perfectly honest, you can be... Because you make no effort, not to be..

MATTHEW: *(looks over at the dining table)* Come on, you're, just upset because I missed dinner...

JUDY: I wasn't upset, I was angry.

MATTHEW: But I couldn't get away, I got caught up in the pub, with the new boss.

JUDY: Anyway, it wasn't you I was angry with, I was angry myself.

MATTHEW: Why?

JUDY: Because, *(gestures toward the bed)* what you thought you witnessed, wasn't about you.

MATTHEW: *(looks surprised)* No..? Then who? Not good old jolly Roger, surely?

JUDY: Don't be ridiculous....

MATTHEW: So you've met someone else?

JUDY: No.

MATTHEW: Then tell me.

JUDY: Mark, of course.

MATTHEW: Mark? Wow! I never saw that coming. *(laughs)* You are joking right? You don't mean our Mark? *(JUDY nods)* But he's gay. Or have you forgotten?

JUDY: No, I haven't. Or that he's fun to be with.

MATTHEW: And I'm not I suppose?

JUDY: As I said, you can be. *(looks over towward the bed and scoffs)*... For about ten percent of the time.

MATTHEW: You've got to be kidding me... Mark? You realise this is crazy?

JUDY: Perhaps... And I'll tell you something else... If he were straight, I'd marry him.

MATTHEW: *(smirks)* This is definitely a wind up... So congratulations, you've succeeded. Now you can drop the act.

JUDY: But it isn't one... I mean it.

MATTHEW: *(smiles)* Sure, of course you do. Now, come on. Put me out of my misery... This is a bad joke, right?

JUDY: I'm afraid it's not.

MATTHEW: But you can't be serious?

JUDY: Why?

MATTHEW: Why? I can think of a million reasons why!

JUDY: I'm sure you can. But, at least with Mark, about ninety percent of the time, there will never be a dull moment...

MATTHEW: And they'll never be any kids either. I admit, I may not be what you consider a fun, but at least we could have children.

JUDY: I'm very fond of you both. But when it comes down to it, we can't choose who we fall in love with, can we?

MATTHEW: Love? But this isn't love, it's madness! *(flustered)* Look, I think better get off this subject.

JUDY: What to? I know, how about what's on the tele tonight? Who knows, if we're lucky, there might be a game of rugby, or even an old cowboy film on...

MATTHEW: Okay, I get it. Look, when I start the new job, I promise, I'll take you out for dinner... Every night if you wish! And instead of watching TV, we can even go to the theatre. Things will be very different, you'll see.

JUDY: You obviously didn't hear what I just said. I mean it, I'm serious.

MATTHEW: *(scoffs)* About Mark? Don't be silly, you can't be... You're just feeling sorry for him, that's all.

JUDY: If anything, I think he feels sorry for me.

145

MATTHEW: You're just deluding yourself. You can't change someone's sexual preferences.

JUDY: Maybe not, but that won't stop me asking him to move in... We can see how things develop from there.

MATTHEW: Remember, when we first met, I said I had something important to tell you about him.

JUDY: And I said, I didn't want to hear... And I still don't.

MATTHEW: Like it or not, it's time you learned the truth about your sweet little Mark.

JUDY: Whatever he's supposed to have done, I couldn't care less.

MATTHEW: It's not what he's done... It's what he is that matters... Now, just hear me out.

JUDY: No, I won't... And if you insist, then I think it best you leave!

MATTHEW: But you must listen to me... It's for your own good!

JUDY: Whatever he's done, neither of us can change, so what's the point in you digging over his past?

MATTHEW: It's not his past, that you should be worried about!

JUDY: Don't you get it? I'm just not interested.

MATTHEW: Never say I didn't try to warn you.

JUDY: Then it seems, I'll just have to take my chances.

MATTHEW: Also, take it from me... When he's no longer around... I'll be back.

JUDY: Then for your sake, I wouldn't bank on it.

MATTHEW: *(becomes angry)* The very thought of you and that queer living together, it's sick... I could kill him!

JUDY: You do realise how crazy that sounds?

MATTHEW: Maybe... But it seems, it's the only way to all stop this.

JUDY: If you really believe that, then I suggest, you do us all a favour and leave. Oh, and while I think of it... don't come back!

MATTHEW: *(calms down, then goes to the door and opens it)* You mean that?

JUDY: Yes, I do.

MATTHEW: *(stares at JUDY)* You do realise, you must be as mad as he is.

JUDY: Hopefully... Then we'll have at least two things in common.

MATTHEW: *(Sarcastically)* What's the other? Knitting?

JUDY: No, it's something I'm beginning to appreciate, is as good as sex... And Mark has in spades!

MATTHEW: Does he indeed... And what is that?

JUDY: It's something you lack... Humour, a sense of humour...

MATTHEW: *(seems puzzled)* What's that got to do with anything?

JUDY: Think about it. When have we ever enjoyed a good laugh together? I mean, over something we both found funny? Or come to that, shared a joke, no matter how stupid, or unfunny...

MATTHEW: Well, if it's a laugh you want, then, I promise you, pretty soon, I'll give you something to really laugh about! *(storms out and slams the door behind him. JUDY picks up a cushion and begins to cry, as she throws it after him)*

END OF SCENE IV

ACT II SCENE V

Daytime. The flat appears empty. There are some cleaning materials on the table in front of the sofa and there is a vacuum cleaner in the middle of the room. MATTHEW enters. So as not to make a noise, he leaves the front door ajar. Walks over to the table and picks up some polish, looks at it, then puts it down. He looks round and walks upstage to the kitchen area.

MATTHEW: *(whispers)* Mark. *(pauses)* Mark? I know you're here. Come on, now! Show yourself. There's no time for silly games. *(goes to the bathroom and tries the door, it appears locked)* Come on! Open this door...

MARK: *(V.O. from the bathroom)* Go away! Please just go away!

MATTHEW: I said 'open it!' Now, don't annoy me...You know, you don't like it when I'm angry.

MARK: *(V.O. from the bathroom)* You're crazy!

MATTHEW: No, it's you that's crazy.

MARK: Judy's told me everything, so there's no way I'm opening this door.

MATTHEW: I promise... I only came here to tell you that you've won... Now, come on, open it before I break it down.

MARK: No... You'd best leave. She'll be back soon.

MATTHEW: Having just seen her get into a taxi with good old Roger, I'd say, that's highly unlikely, wouldn't you?

MARK: Even so, I'm not coming out till she gets back.

MATTHEW: If you come out, I'll fix us a drink. Then we can sit down like old mates, and sort this mess out. I admit it, I made mistakes. But be fair, we both did.

MARK: *(V.O. behind the bathroom door)* I know what your up to, so your wasting you're time... Remember, I know your tricks!

MATTHEW: *(starts to get annoyed and bangs the bathroom door with his fist)* I said, come out! Now just do it! Don't force me to come in there. If you do, it'll get very nasty! *(waits for an answer)* Okay, have it your way. On the count of three, I'm coming in... one... two ...

MARK: *(V.O. from the bathroom)* Alright! I'm coming out. *(MATTHEW rattles the handle and we hear the sound of the key unlocking. As the door opens, MATTHEW stands at the entrance. The audience will see MARK'S reflection in a bathroom mirror)*

MATTHEW: Why were you hiding? You must know by now, you can't escape me.

MARK: *(V.O.)* What are you up to? You're not meant to be here.

MATTHEW: I'm here, to put an end to her delusions about you... You nearly blew it for both of us.

MARK: Me? But how?

MATTHEW: By losing that silly bag of yours.

MARK: But I didn't lose it.

MATTHEW: If she had used that key, the game would have been up.

MARK: But she didn't, did she?

MATTHEW: You do realise, Roger took your bag on purpose?

MARK: Then you can hardly blame me?

MATTHEW: Really? You were the idiot who left it lying around.

MARK: Yes, but there's no harm done. He brought it back, didn't he?

MATTHEW: I'm sure he was onto you from the start.

MARK: Maybe, but he hasn't yet made the connection. Trust me, it's okay... He's never seen me go in there.

MATTHEW: If he's been in there, he's bound to have seen your clothes.

MARK: Maybe, I don't know. Don't confuse me. You can't put all the blame on me. You are as much to blame, as I am.

MATTHEW: Either way, he's suspicious. I've seen him lurking in the corridor. In a way, I wish he had exposed you... Then I wouldn't have to be here now.

MARK: I don't understand. I've said, I'll be more careful...What more do you want from me?

MATTHEW: How about my life back?

MARK: Oh, please, you're insane,.You always have been.

MATTHEW: Perhaps, but this time you've gone too far.

MARK: Have I really? Remember, I'm the one who got us in here.

MATTHEW: But you were supposed to disappear, the moment she fell in love with me. Not make her fall in love with you!

MARK: I didn't... You did that, by being your usual dull self.

MATTHEW: I can't understand it. You're just meant to be just the amusing freak show... But now she's in love with you.

MARK: No, you've got it all wrong. She loves us both...

MATTHEW: Both?

MARK: It's so obvious... In fact, it couldn't be more perfect. You, the great lover! And me, the amusing companion... There's no reason we can't all be friends.

MATTHEW: But it's you she loves...

MARK: Nonsense! She just thinks she does. What she really wants is someone who can fulfil all her needs.

MATTHEW: Meaning?

MARK: If you make more of an effort, And pay her some attention, it could still be you.

MATTHEW: Don't you think I already know that? But I get paralysed with guilt, knowing I'm lying to her.

MARK: Then, tell her the truth... You owe her that at least.

MATTHEW: Believe me, I've tried more than once, but I always get so bloody tongue-tied.

MARK: But why?

MATTHEW: Because I love her...

MARK: Well, snap! We both do...

MATTHEW: I just can't bear the thought of hurting her.

MARK: *(smirks)* But it seems, you already have.

MATTHEW: It's so unfair!

MARK: Then, what are we going to do about it?

MATTHEW: We? Nothing. You won't be here... You'll be gone.

MARK: *(scoffs)* Arn't you forgetting something? Whether I'm here or not, you'll still need me.

MATTHEW: I wouldn't bank on it.

MARK: I'm afraid I would, because you always will.

MATTHEW: I'm sure, in time, even I could learn to tell a few silly jokes.

MARK: If you think that's all it is, then go for it. Give it a try.

MATTHEW: Yes, I will...

MARK: You know, I really pity you. I can't imagine how much you must loathe standing in my shadow.

MATTHEW: Don't worry, you won't have to imagine for much longer!

MARK: *(chuckles)* You've got to admit... It is ironic.

MATTHEW: What is?

MARK: That it was her, that messed up your little scheme.

MATTHEW: No, it was you... By hanging around too long.

MARK: Only because she needs me.

MATTHEW: What a joke. Believe me, once you've gone, she'll soon get over it.

MARK: But I've no intention of going anywhere.

MATTHEW: You're only deluding yourself... She no longer needs you in her life... She's got me now.

MARK: Perhaps she doesn't, but you do.

MATTHEW: No, I don't! Perhaps in reality, I never did!

MARK: let's face it, you lost touch with reality years ago.

MATTHEW: You're right... And for far too long, but not anymore.

MARK: *(smirks)* Look, why don't you, just for once in your life, be honest with yourself and admit you need me.

MATTHEW: *(Scoffs)* As honest as you are, right? Now, just do us both a favour... and go! Leave before it's too late. Before I...

MARK: Before you what?

MATTHEW: I'm begging you... For the last time, get out of my life... Just go!

MARK: If one of us has to go, it's not going to be me.

MATTHEW: Then you're giving me no choice... I'm going to have to do what I should have done years ago.

MARK: *(scoffs)* And what is that exactly?

MATTHEW: Kill you, of course!

MARK: *(laughs)* Oh, please, do you realise how pathetic that sounds? Don't be ridiculous, you know you can't do that.

MATTHEW: I can at least going to try.

MARK: *(walks slowly toward MARK)* I warn you Matthew, don't even attempt it... You'll come off worse, I promise.

MATTHEW: Perhaps, but either way, this has to end and end now... I'm sorry! *(We see a vague scuffle as the bathroom door closes. Then we hear a piercing scream and the sound of the mirror shattering)*

BLACKOUT
END OF SCENE V

ACT II SCENE VI

Living room, daytime.

(MATTHEW is in the kitchen area, with his back to the audience. He is naked. The room looks a mess, curtains ripped down, ornaments broken and photos torn up and strewn on the floor etc. Anything that MARK has added is smashed. The door slowly opens and KATE enters. She looks over at MATTHEW)

KATE: *(Surprised at seeing him naked)* Oh, hello. Sorry, the door was open. I did ring first, but no one answered. *(KATE'S eye line is on MATTHEW'S bottom)* Oh, my God. Judy's right, you really are beautiful. You must be Matthew? I've heard so much about you. Now I can see what she sees in you. *(looks his naked body)* It's funny, I feel I already know you. *(MATTHEW is still hunched over the sink with his back to the audience. He doesn't reply)* I'm Kate. Judy's mother's youngest sister. I just popped in on the off chance. *(goes to sit on the sofa and for the first time she registers the mess)* Good God! What has been going on here? This place looks like a bomb hit it. *(KATE goes over to the kitchen area. As she walks towards MATTHEW he turns around. KATE at first, is distracted by his front view. Before noticing, MATTHEW is holding a large piece of broken mirror with blood dripping from it. She then notices some blood stained clothing on the sink. MATTHEW's arm is also bleed-

ing) What on earth…? *(MATTHEW drops the mirror and starts to wrap his bloody arm in a piece of clothing)* What happened to your arm, you're bleeding? And who made all this mess? *(MATTHEW doesn't reply)* I asked who made all this mess? What's been going on here? Answer me. *(pauses as she looks at MATTHEW's naked body, then takes hold of his arm)* Let me look at that. *(KATE looks at the piece of cloth wrapped around it)* Hold on? I recognise this ghastly pattern. *(looks in the kitchen and notices the chute for the rubbish is open and some of MARK's clothing is hanging out. She goes over and examines it)* Out of interest, where is your queer friend? *(looks around)* My God... You haven't? Have you? *(MATTHEW doesn't react)* I don't believe it! What a scandal this will be, if this gets out. Especially for me! I'll have to be a witness! And my poor little Judy, it's her flat. I should have warned her to get references. I knew from the start he was up to no good. By the look of things, he certainly put up a fight. *(KATE sees a candlestick on the floor)* Whacked him with that did you? *(KATE again pauses, as she stares back at MAT-THEW's naked body)* Obviously, it was self defence. Personally, I would have paid someone to get rid of him. Now, let me think... We can't just gloss over this. *(KATE picks up the candlestick)* You could say, you were defending yourself. What Judy ever saw in him, I'll never know. For some unknown reason, he mesmerised her. *(KATE looks down at MATTHEW's crotch)* Like a mongoose with a snake. *(KATE notices MATTHEW's arm is bleeding even more)* Oh, dear, I can't stand the sight of blood. I think I'm going to faint. *(KATE puts her arm on MATTHEW's shoulder to steady herself. MATTHEW puts a hand on her neck and looks at her. At first, KATE appears nervous, then relaxes)* I must say it's been hours since I've felt the strong hands of a young man caressing my neck. *(MATTHEW suddenly drops his hand and moves away)* Look, you may think me callous, if I suggest it, but at the risk of you thinking my morals are somewhat flexible, I think I've thought of a way out of this. *(MAT-THEW just stares vacantly)* Okay, well, I'll just throw this out there, and you say what you think... Now Judy has gone to that new Hockney exhibition. Which means, it gives us at least a couple of hours to clean this place up and get out of here. Apart from that broken mirror, It'll be like nothing has happened. *(MATTHEW still doesn't react. KATE walks over to the clothing hanging out of the rubbish chute)* I assume, he's down there? *(pats MATTHEW on the bottom)* After we're done here, you can come back to my house and lie low. *(She throws more of MARK'S clothes down the chute)* I'll take care of everything. *(looks him up and down)* Everything from your cuff -links to your underpants. But somehow, I don't think you'll be needing those. So it's a deal...Yes? *(MATTHEW doesn't answer, instead he goes to the bathroom, picks up a towel and wraps it round his waist)* Well, let's say an arrangement... It sounds less business like. For my part, I'll deny ever seeing you here. I'll tell them I saw Mark smashing the mirror, before he ran off saying he was never coming back. From what I gather, no one knows where he lives, so the police can't check. *(KATE leans forward to kiss MATTHEW, but he pulls back in disgust)* What's wrong? Listen my dear, you're in no position to be choosy. I may not be as young as Judy, but at least I know how to make love, like a real woman, not a silly little girl. So what's it to be? A life of luxury? Or a life sentence? *(MATTHEW just stares at her)* Look you stupid little bugger, I'm offering you your freedom... more than that; me! *(MATTHEW still doesn't react)* Now, make up your mind, but before you answer, remember, if it's a no, I'll make sure you go down for murder. *(MATTHEW begins to throw the remnants of MARK's possessions down the chute)* Don't do that! That's evidence! I really must be more stupid, than I am selfish. I don't need you, I can pick up twenty boys like you any night... and not all of them want paying. Right, I'm ringing the police. *(goes over to the phone)* You are as pathetic as he was. How did you do it? Creep up from behind him while he was cleaning? What a coward you are! A fit guy like you, he wouldn't have stood a chance. *(KATE sees a large piece of bathroom mirror on the kitchen sink)* Of course, now it all makes sense. *(KATE picks up the piece of bloodstained mirror)* Messy, but quick, eh? Ah, that's why you're naked, no blood on your clothes? *(MATTHEW just stares vacantly)* I hope it was all worth it! A long stretch in prison, just because that dreadful Mark had our little Judy's affection.

MATTHEW: *(at the mention of JUDY'S name, MATTHEW looks over at KATE)* Judy?

KATE: That's right... I know all about it. The poor girl was on the phone sobbing her heart out. If you ask me, she's demented. He would have been useless as a lover, she'd be better off with you. But then, there's no accounting for taste.... So, my beauty, it seems, you've done all this for nothing. Judy's hardly going to fall madly in love with his killer. Instead, she's going to hate you... and I mean, really hate you. She relied on that little queer for everything... *(KATE smirks)* Well, almost everything. But then she always got her priorities wrong. *(MATTHEW suddenly bangs his fist on the kitchen sink)* Oh, dear, have I touched a raw nerve? *(KATE goes to pick up the phone. As she does, MATTHEW tries to stop her. KATE reaches for a beer glass to hit him with. MATTHEW grabs her and they struggle. He pushes her onto the floor and holds her down, as he takes the glass from her hand. Then MATTHEW clasps the glass with both hands, raises his arms high above his head and lets out an eerie high-pitched moan)*

MATTHEW: Maaaark! *(He brings the glass down toward KATE'S face. KATE screams. Just before the glass reaches her face, MATTHEW stops and looks at her)*

KATE: Don't. Please don't! Let me go, I won't tell anyone, I promise. *(MATTHEW looks at KATE and squeezes the glass until it breaks and blood begins to drip onto her face. KATE screams again and passes out. MATTHEW stands up, gets a cushion and puts it under her head. He then takes a towel and sits in one of the armchairs. After a couple of seconds, the silence is broken by the sound of a key being turned in the front door)*

JUDY: *(O.S)* Thanks, Roger, it's been a lovely day.

ROGER: *(O.S)* Glad you enjoyed it.

JUDY: *(opens the door giggling)* They were too generous with that free champagne, I feel quite woozy. *(She looks around)* Good grief, I can't be that drunk! The state of this place... Roger. Roger! *(ROGER enters)*

ROGER: Oh, dear! *(As ROGER surveys the scene, JUDY becomes excitable. ROGER walks over at KATE lying on the floor, crouches down and checks her pulse)* At least, we're not too late.

JUDY: What on earth has happened? Will she be alright?

ROGER: *(ROGER gently taps KATE)* I think so. Quickly, get a dish cloth and dip it in cold water. Kate... Kate! *(JUDY brings him the wet cloth. ROGER places it on Kate's head)* Kate! *(KATE slowly opens her eyes)* It's all right, she's coming round.

KATE: *(Still drowsy, KATE looks surprised at seeing ROGER)* Roger.. It's you? I must have fainted...

ROGER: How you feeling?

KATE: *(ROGER takes KATE'S pulse again)* Oh, please don't fuss! I'm fine. Nothing a gin & tonic wouldn't cure.

JUDY: *(looks over at MATTHEW who is just sitting staring blankly)* Mathew! What on earth's been going on? *(MATHEW doesn't react)*

KATE: *(points to MATTHEW)* You won't believe it, but that bastard's killed Mark.

JUDY: Don't be ridiculous!

KATE: *(KATE slowly sits up)* I'm serious. Look around you, there's blood everywhere. He must have crept up behind him and hit him with that. *(points to the candlestick)*

JUDY: Don't be silly, Matthew wouldn't do that...

KATE: Oh, wouldn't he? Well, a quick newsflash, he has.

JUDY: *(appears horrified)* Matthew is this true? *(MATTHEW still doesn't react)*

KATE: What's more, he stabbed him with that mirror to finish the job. *(KATE points to the shard of broken mirror)*

JUDY: My God! This can't be happening?

KATE: It isn't, it's already happened.

JUDY: Oh, come on, be serious, where is Mark?

KATE: I should imagine, down that chute, with the rest of the rubbish. *(points to MATTHEW)* He was pushing the last bits of his clothing down it, when I arrived.

ROGER: Judging by the state of this place, there must have been one hell of a struggle. *(goes over to the chute and lifts out something and looks at it, then holds it up)* Looks like a pair of braces.

JUDY: *(looks relieved)* Then they can't be Mark's. He never wears braces, he wears those flashy designer belts.

KATE: Yes, he always was vulgar.

JUDY: What's all this? *(picks up something from the floor)* It's rice! See...? It's everywhere.

ROGER: Rice? *(pulls something else out of the chute)* Yuck! Well look at this.

JUDY: What on earth is it?

ROGER: It looks like hair matted in blood... Yes, it's definitely hair, human hair. *(examines it further)* And from what I can make out, it's Mark's.

JUDY: How can it be?

ROGER: Because it's blond... and it's dyed.

JUDY: No.. You're mistaken... Anyway, his was natural.

ROGER: I don't think so. *(looks into the chute again)* Hold on, there's something else... It's Mark's bag.

JUDY: That's strange? He wouldn't go anywhere without that.

ROGER: *(unzips MARK'S bag and dips into it)* And what have we in here? Ah! His contact lenses.

JUDY: Then it's definitely not him... He didn't wear contact lenses.

ROGER: Yes he did! He wore these, *(shows JUDY)* brown ones!

JUDY: *(confused)* But why would he?

ROGER: I think you'll find it was Mark who had blue eyes. *(brings out something very gungy and unrecognisable)* This really does look gruesome.

KATE: What on earth is it?

ROGER: It could well be human ... *(takes it out of the chute and puts it on the kitchen sink, then wipes his hands with a tea towel)*

KATE: It looks revolting. I think I just might have to faint again.

JUDY: *(becomes upset)* Roger, now stop this! Just call the police.

ROGER: *(ROGER continues searching)* No, not yet.

JUDY: *(still distraught looks over at MATTHEW)* Bur Matthew why? How could you do this? *(MATTHEW doesn't react)* Answer me!

ROGER: Now, Judy, just calm down!

JUDY: *(looks over at KATE)* And why is he sitting there naked?

KATE: To avoid getting blood on his clothes, why else? After killing Mark, he would have dressed and walked out of here without a bloodstain on him... If I hadn't have arrived when I did, he'd have been long gone. *(gets a drink and settles back down)*

ROGER: *(eyes KATE suspiciously)* I don't think that was the reason he took his clothes off.

KATE: Yes, well... I do tend to have that effect on men. Now call the police, before he comes out of his trance, or whatever he is in.

ROGER: Not yet, just bear with me.

KATE: *(smirks)* But he could attack us, at any minute!

ROGER: *(looks over at MATTHEW)* He seems far too traumatised to do anything... Just tell me exactly what happened when you arrived?

KATE: He was like he is now... In another world. So I did what any sensible person would do: I picked up the phone to ring the police... And that's when he attacked me.

ROGER: You didn't say anything?

KATE: Don't be silly, I didn't get a chance.

JUDY: *(As JUDY looks over at MATTHEW she bursts into tears and becomes hysterical)* Why? Why would you do this? It makes no sense... answer me! *(ROGER goes to JUDY and gently shakes her. As he does, MATTHEW turns and looks over at them and makes a whining sound)*

ROGER: *(looks at him)* It's all right, I'm not hurting her. Judy, stop it! Now just calm down and pull yourself together. Now take some deep breaths. *(takes a few deep breaths and calms down)*

JUDY: I'm sorry.

ROGER: Am I right in thinking that last night, you two had one heck of a row?

JUDY: *(surprised)* Yes, but how?

ROGER: I do live across the hall, remember? And you were shouting. From what I gathered, it was about Mark.

JUDY: It usually is. I told him, I was going to ask Mark to move in... and who knows, one day even marry him.

KATE: Has everyone gone completely mad?

ROGER: And that's when he got really angry?

JUDY: Yes, that's when you must have heard us shouting...

ROGER: Well, then it seems you gave him no choice.

JUDY: What on earth do you mean?

ROGER: I mean, then he had to kill Mark.

KATE: What? So now, it's her fault?

ROGER: In a way, yes. You see, Matthew never bargained for the possibility of you loving Mark.

KATE: Now, stop all this nonsense. Just ring the police and be done with it. You're sounding as crazy as he is. *(gestures toward MATTHEW)*

ROGER: Matthew's not crazy, he's just lost.

KATE: Well don't try and find him.

JUDY: It's me that's lost. I don't understand any of this. It make no sense. *(stands up)* Kate's right, we should call the police.

ROGER: I have a feeling that won't be necessary.

KATE: What d'you mean?

ROGER: Of course, I'd need to get a second opinion. But my guess is, he's suffering from some form of personality disorder...

KATE: Well, that's an understatement! Ring the police! We're sitting in a room with a maniac. *(looks over at ROGER)* Maybe two!

ROGER: *(smiles)* I don't think so, but granted Matthew does need treatment.

KATE: That's one way of putting it. He's a killer for god's sake! *(goes to dial the police).*

ROGER: *(ltakes the reciever from her hand and replaces it. He then goes over to the kitchen and picks up what he took from the chute)* Before you ring the police, take a closer look at these.

KATE: No! I couldn't bear to. I admit I loathed him, but I didn't wish him dead... Well, not this way.

ROGER: Now, come on. *(shows KATE the hair)* It's only Mark's hair.

KATE: Oh, please. It looks revolting!

JUDY: For goodness sake, Roger! Whatever you're playing at... Just stop it!

ROGER: I'm not playing. I promise you, it's for your own good. Just look closer. You see the hair belongs to Mark, alright...

JUDY: But it can't be his... Mark wasn't bald.

ROGER: You're right, he wasn't.

JUDY: Then how can it be his hair?

ROGER: I didn't say it was, I said, it belonged to him. See, it's been dyed. *(shows JUDY).*

JUDY: Then it isn't his. He told me himself, his was natural.

KATE: You are so gullible dear. *(picks up something else and shows it to KATE)* What on earth's that?

ROGER: Now take a look at this.

JUDY: Yuck! What is it?

ROGER: By the looks of it, human flesh. (*shows it to JUDY*)

JUDY: You can't be serious? Take it away!

KATE: *(ROGER shows it to KATE)* Yuck! No, thanks, I've had lunch!

ROGER: Judy, just feel it... Go on feel it. It's not real, I promise *(offers it to JUDY to feel)*

JUDY: No way! whatever it is, it's disgusting... I think I'm going to be sick!

ROGER: You won't be... (*places her hand on the it)* See? It's just latex! Mark used it to create the illusion of having a fat stomach.

KATE: Yes, well he did have quite a gut on him.

ROGER: No, he didn't. Neither was he blond... He wore that wig, made of Asian hair, that's been dyed...

JUDY: So Mark did wear a wig?

ROGER: Yes. And this? It's a piece of his fake latex stomach.

KATE: Well, it certainly looks human enough...

ROGER: Because it's been painted a flesh colour. And that explains why there's rice everywhere. That's what he used to stuff it with...

KATE: But why rice?

ROGER: To give the appearance of natural movement. Granted a bit crude, but it worked. *(holds up the braces)* And these little darlings are what he used to hold it all in place... The reason for all this paraphernalia goes back to your advert.

JUDY: For a cleaner? Now I'm really lost...

ROGER: You see, it was Matthew who saw your ad in the shop window. But instead of applying for the job himself, he sent Mark.

KATE: Why would he do that?

ROGER: Lack of confidence.

JUDY: Oh, come off it. Confidence was the last thing Matt was lacking in...

ROGER: Believe me, underneath that veneer of charm and self confidence, I think you'll find, he's extremely shy.

JUDY: I don't uderstand?

KATE: *(looks over at MATTHEW)* Me neither, after all, he's got a lot going for him... Underneath that towel that is.

JUDY: But why?

ROGER: As to why, I have no idea. It could be a combination of many things.

JUDY: Such as?

ROGER: Who knows? Maybe he's suffered some form of emotional or physical trauma... The loss of a loved one perhaps. Or maybe, when he was younger, he was abused in some way... I've no idea. There can be a number of reasons that might have triggered his condition.

JUDY: Mark did say, when Matthew was a boy, his father used to beat him.

ROGER: There we are, that's is reason enough for anyone to lack self esteem... Thus making it nigh impossible to make friends and so become lonely... In his case, desperately lonely.

JUDY: But that was years ago.

ROGER: Yes, and in all that time, loneliness would easily have lead to despair.

JUDY: But he wasn't lonely... He had a friend... he had Mark.

ROGER: In a way... Yes, I suppose he did...

KATE: There we are then... As I thought, you're talking nonsense.

ROGER: I'm not... Loneliness can be a far more complex emotion than people imagine... It can lead to a downward spiral... can often prove to be a killer.

KATE: Ah! So he did kill Mark?

ROGER: I didn't say that...

KATE: Then what are you saying?

ROGER: For some, their imagination can be the only escape from despair.

JUDY: Oh, poor Matthew...

KATE: 'Poor Matthew!' You've got to be kidding!

JUDY: Kate, just shut up for a moment and hear him out..

KATE: Ah, so now we're back to square one!

ROGER: You're right, Matthew did have a friend, a sort of secret friend, who in his deperation, he created. More accurately, an alternate persona.

KATE: And what's that when it's at home?

ROGER: An alternative personality, which, at times, became so real to him that it took over completely... It's not that uncommon.

JUDY: So you're saying he has a split personality?

170

ROGER: Sort of... But as I say, it's a little more complicated than that. There are of course several variations of, what is also known, as a Multiple Personality Disorder.

JUDY: Meaning what exactly?

ROGER: Meaning, in many respects, we are no different to him.

KATE: Now, you really are talking rubbish!

ROGER: Be honest, who in this room hasn't, at one time or another, been guilty of talking to themselves?

KATE: I'll give you that. I do... It's the only time I get a compliment!

JUDY: But surely, that's different?

ROGER: Not really. All of us have different facets, alternate sides to our personalites, both good and bad. How we project ourselves depends on a variety of factors. Our moods, or the stituation we find ourselves in. And, when needed, we put on one of our many different faces... As easy as donning a mask...

KATE: I would agree with you there... All my friends are cetainly two faced... If not not more!

JUDY: But how does that explain all this? *(gestures to the room)*

ROGER: What happened here was never part of the plan.

JUDY: Plan? What plan?

ROGER: To kill Mark.

JUDY: So he has killed him?

ROGER: Let's all just step back a bit, shall we? *(looks at MAT-THEW)* What do we actually have here? Someone, whose inability to make friends made their loneliness so unbearable, that in order to escape from it; they used the only thing left at their disposal...

KATE: Which was?

ROGER: Their imagination!

JUDY: But to what end?

ROGER: To imagine they had a friend... Who, over time, they began to believe was real... As did Matthew, when he created Mark.

KATE: Mark? Well, if that is true, why, of all things, did he create that horrible creature?

ROGER: Because Mark was everything Matthew wasn't. Flamboyant, extrovert... Confident, outgoing... More importantly, someone he could hide behind... What we are seeing here are the remnants of that friendship. *(points to the hair and fake stomach)*

JUDY: This plan you mentioned? What had that to do with me?

ROGER: Don't you see? That's the real reason he created Mark... To find someone to have a relationship with... Someone who could eventually love him. And Mark did just that, he found you.

JUDY: Me?

ROGER: Yes, *(looks around the room)* the plan was, once Mark found the right girl, he would make himself indispensable. Then,

172

when the time was right, Mark would introduce Matthew. At that point, Mark would quietly disappear... forever. *(looks over at MATTHEW)* The problem began, when you appeared to favour Mark over Matthew.

JUDY: But I didn't...

ROGER: Maybe not, but you told him you did. What's more, you appeared to make a choice between them.

JUDY: I just wanted Matthew to be more like Mark, that's all. I only said that to annoy him.

ROGER: And you succeeded.

JUDY: But I couldn't have made a choice, even if I had wanted to.

ROGER: But he didn't know that. Don't you see? The idea of living out his relationship and making love to you, as Mark, disgusted him. So he had to kill him off.

KATE: And good riddance, he managed that at least.

ROGER: But he hasn't... *(looks over at MATTHEW, who is still sitting cross legged in the armchair, staring out into the auditorium)*

JUDY: Meaning?

ROGER: With time and a lot of patience, no doubt, Matthew's confidence will grow, and his dependence on Mark subside. *(looks at JUDY)* Especially with your help.

JUDY: My help?

ROGER: Unless I'm wrong, you were and still are in love with both of them?

JUDY: But...?

ROGER: You said that you couldn't choose between them. Well, if that really is the case, you should thank Kate. She saved both of them.

KATE: Me?

ROGER: By arriving when you did, it wasn't a murder you had just missed; it was a suicide you had prevented. A few minutes later and Matthew would have been dead.

JUDY: And Mark?

ROGER: Mark, too. You see, when Matthew saw his reflection in the bathroom mirror, all he could see was Mark. It was in his attempt to destroy him, when the battle between them really began.

KATE: Battle?

ROGER: Matthew tried to destroy anything of Mark's he could lay his hands on. His clothes, make-up, wig, whatever, and dispose of it down that chute.

JUDY: But why?

ROGER: That way, there would be no tangible evidence that Mark had ever existed. But of course, that didn't work... Mark was still there, reflected in the bathroom mirror, and so he smashed it. Then he took off his own clothes and ripped them up.

KATE: None of that makes sense, I think I'll stick to my own theory... He's a raving lunatic!

ROGER: No, he's not. Don't you see? By doing that, there would be no more costumes for either of them to hide behind. It was only in his nakedness, Mathew realised it wasn't going to be that easy. Mark's reflection was still there in the shards of that shattered mirror. *(picks up a large piece of bloodied mirror and looks at KATE)* If you hadn't turned up when you did, I have a feeling this was put aside to finish the job.

KATE: It all sounds very far-fetched.

JUDY: Yes, it does... How can you be so certain of this?

ROGER: The key.

JUDY: What key?

ROGER: To the boiler room.

KATE: Here we go again. *(pours herself a drink)* Now I'm really confused. What boiler room?

ROGER: The one down in the basement. *(turns to JUDY)* Remember when I accidentally picked up Mark's bag, instead of my baccy pouch?

JUDY: Yes, there was a mix up.

ROGER: There was no mix up. The truth is, I borrowed it.

KATE: Oh no, not another one into handbags.

ROGER: No, I was just curious, as to why the key was so important to Mark. If you remember, he never let it out of his sight.

JUDY: That's true, he did get very upset when it went missing.

ROGER: Because he was worried that I may have discovered what it opened... And he was right.

KATE: *(fluffs up her blooded cushion and settles down with her drink)* Curiouser and curiouser... But do get to the point.. *(looks at her hands)* I've been lying here so long, I'm getting liver spots!

ROGER: What I discovered in the boiler room, confirmed my suspicions... Matthew and Mark were the same person.

JUDY: What? But that can't be... Of course their not!

ROGER: I'm afraid they are...

JUDY: Don't be ridiculous. D'you remember that night you returned Mark's bag?

ROGER: I do indeed.

JUDY: Well, Mark had just left through the kitchen window, because he thought it was Matthew at the door.

ROGER: No, Mark guessed it was me. In a way, I played into his hands. For him, it was a perfect ploy. He wound you up to expect Matthew, but instead, it was me. Then when Matthew did appear, he really did take you by surprise.

KATE: But why didn't you say something before?

ROGER: Because I wasn't sure what he was up to. Professional curiosity I suppose.

KATE: But I thought you were a gynaecologist not a psychiatrist.

ROGER: I am. But I did a course in psychology as a student. Believe me, it helps to be a bit of both in my job.

KATE: Yes, I suppose so. In your business, it must be refreshing to see things from a different angle, so to speak.

JUDY: Why didn't you tell me all this sooner? He could have killed me.

ROGER: You were never in any danger. Matthew was only a danger to himself. Besides, *(opens the door and points into the hallway off stage)* I was never far from that door. Since I've been on holiday, I've hardly left my flat.

KATE: *(Smirks)* How very gallant. So what is the big secret of the boiler room?

ROGER: Clothes... Mark's and Matthew's. That's where they... Or should I say he, *(points at MATTHEW)* changed and reappeared, as one or the other. Its location allowed him to do so in a matter of minutes, that's why he stored them there... And that's why he kept it locked.

JUDY: But you still had the key to the boiler room the night Matthew first appeared. So how could Mark have changed?

ROGER: I left it, as always, as it used to be - unlocked. I wanted him to know I had been there.

177

KATE: *(looks over at MATTHEW)* My, my, he's a proper little Jekyll and Hyde...

ROGER: He's certainly no Mr Hyde... He's not dangerous.

KATE: You've got to be kidding. He tried to kill me!

ROGER: I very much doubt that.

KATE: I'm serious. When I tried to ring the police he went ballistic.

ROGER: Really? What was the last thing you remember, before you passed out?

JUDY: The last thing I remember was, he was screaming Mark's name... You should have seen his eyes, they were literally popping out of his head.

ROGER: Well, if he screamed Mark's name, it wasn't you he was trying to kill, was it? You just got in the way.

KATE: *(sarcastically)* Oh, thanks for your concern. Anyway, if all this nonsense you're telling us is true, then why did he create such an outrageous, sissy as Mark? Why not a normal, straight man?

ROGER: Because Mark was no threat to a woman living on her own. Judy would have thought twice about employing a straight man.

KATE: Not me, I only ever employ straight men. *(KATE vamps ROGER)* There always be a job vacancy for you, Roger.

ROGER: *(lights up his pipe)* Yes, well, while we're on the subject, I think it's only fair to point out... I'm gay.

KATE: *(JUDY and KATE Look surprised)* Really? Are you sure you don't mean you're just jolly, or happy or something?

ROGER: No, just gay. English is a living, an amazingly adaptable language.

KATE: What a waste! Just when I thought it was safe to get off the sofa...

JUDY: I knew there was something, but I'd never have guessed... Why didn't you tell me you were gay?

ROGER: You never asked?

KATE: *(whinces as she sips some sherry)* Disgusting!
(ROGER looks offended) Not you, this stuff. Is nobody straight anymore?

ROGER: He is. *(points to MATTHEW)*

KATE: That's a relief. Okay, allowing for all this madness, answer me this: When he read the ad, how did he know whether Judy was going to be attractive?

ROGER: Pure fluke... Mathew was in the shop, when she placed the ad. Think about it. Why d'you think, nobody else applied for the job? Because that ad was removed from the window.

JUDY: Then what happened to it?

ROGER: When I asked the shopkeeper why he no longer displayed it, he said that Judy's boyfriend had returned and cancelled it.

JUDY: My boyfriend?

ʃROGER: He obviously thought you were together. *(walks over to MATTHEW and whispers)* Mark? *(steps back and in a normal voice)* Matthew...? *(raises his voice)* Matthew! *(still gets no response, so signals to JUDY to try)*

JUDY: *(kneels down in front of MATTHEW)* Mark... Mark? *(ROGER nods to her to try again)* Mark! *(MATTHEW doesnt react)*

ROGER: *(whispers to JUDY)* Try Matthew...

JUDY: Matthew? *(MATTHEW doesn't react.)* Matthew... Matthew it's me. *(MATTHEW still doesn't react, so JUDY takes his hand and gently squeezes it)* It's me... It's Judy. *(Very slowly MATTHEW turns and looks at JUDY. As he does, we see he has a faint trace of a smile)*

ROGER: *(looks over at KATE)* Well, it seems at least one good thing has come out of all this...

KATE: Oh really? And what is that exactly?

ROGER: *(looks over at the red leather chairs)* Unlike those chairs, as far as Mathew and Mark are concered, she no longer has to make a choice.

(JUDY straightens MATTHEW's towel, kisses him on the cheek and then hugs him. As the lights fade, David Cassidy's song 'Daydreamer' begins to play)

Allan Warren

CURTAIN

The Matching Pair - Part 2: Double Act

Allan Warren

www.ingramcontent.com/pod-product-compliance
Lightning Source LLC
Chambersburg PA
CBHW071531040426
42452CB00008B/979